Y0-BRV-373

THE IDEA OF DIFFICULTY IN LITERATURE

SUNY Series, Literacy, Culture, and Learning:
Theory and Practice

Alan C. Purves, Editor

THE IDEA OF DIFFICULTY
IN LITERATURE

Edited by
Alan C. Purves

State University of New York Press

Most of the chapters in this volume were prepared under a grant to the Center for the Learning and Teaching of Literature, University at Albany, State University of New York. The grant was Number G008720278, which is cosponsored by the U.S. Department of Education, Office of Educational Research and Improvement (OERI/ED) and by the National Endowment for the Arts (NEA). The opinions expressed in this volume do not necessarily reflect the position or policy of OERI/ED or NEA, and no official endorsement of either agency should be inferred.

"A Narrow Fellow in the Grass" is reprinted by permission of the publishers and the Trustees of Amherst College from *The Poems of Emily Dickinson*, Thomas H. Johnson, ed., Cambridge, Mass.: The Belknap Press of Harvard University Press, copyright 1951, 1955, 1979, 1983 by the President and Fellows of Harvard College.

"Buffalo Bill's" is reprinted from TULIPS & CHIMNEYS by E. E. Cummings, edited by George James Firmage, by permission of Liveright Publishing Corporation. Copyright © 1923, 1925 and renewed 1951, 1953 by E. E. Cummings. Copyright © 1973, 1976 by the Trustees for the E. E. Cummings Trust. Copyright © 1973, 1976 by George James Firmage.

Published by
State University of New York Press, Albany

© 1991   State University of New York

All rights reserved

Printed in the United States of America

No part of this book may be used or reproduced
in any manner whatsoever without written permission
except in the case of brief quotations embodied in
critical articles and reviews.

For information, address State University of New York
Press, State University Plaza, Albany, N.Y. 12246

Production by Dana Foote
Marketing by Theresa A. Swierzowski

Library of Congress Cataloging-in-Publication Data

The Idea of Difficulty in Literature / edited by Alan C. Purves.
        p. cm.—(SUNY series, literacy, culture, and learning)
    Includes bibliographical references and index.
    ISBN 0–7914–0673–3 (CH : acid-free).—ISBN 0–7914–0674–1 (PB : acid-free)
    1. Reader-response criticism. 2. Criticism, Textual.
3. Literature—Study and teaching. 4. Canon (Literature)
    I. Purves, Alan C., 1931– . II. Series: SUNY series on literacy, culture, and learning.
PN98.R38I34 1991
801'.95—dc20   90–43101
                                                                          CIP

10 9 8 7 6 5 4 3 2 1

CONTENTS

Introduction

Alan C. Purves

When the reviewers greet a novel by Thomas Pyncheon, they refer to him as a "difficult" or "obscure" writer. When reviewers comment on a new novel by Stephen King, they may use various adjectives, but not those two. As teachers of literature in English, we know that *Finnegans Wake* by James Joyce is difficult; we know that *Peter Rabbit* by Beatrix Potter is easy. We know that in the 1930s even sophisticated readers found T. S. Eliot difficult, but today's readers have less trouble. Conversely, for many college students a novel of Trollope's or one by Dickens is considered difficult, but in their day they were light general reading. But what makes these texts shift in their category?

The texts clearly have not changed; have the readers? What is it that changes over time and what is it that varies within an era? Is there some objective criterion for determining the difficulty of a work of literature? In the field of reading, formulas are often used to determine something called "readability," formulas based on word and sentence length as well as on counts of word frequency. They seem to work with nonliterary texts, but do these formulas really hold up when one deals with poetry, drama, or fiction? Many of William Blake's lyrics would be low on a readability formula, but many readers would find them difficult.

Perhaps we might better consider difficulty less from an objective perspective, but from a constructivist one. Such a view would suggest that difficulty is an aspect of the individual's estimate of the nature of the object and that individual's estimate of her or his capacity to deal with the object. When a fourteen-year-old boy says of a story "That's a childish story, written for younger kids.... I mean I don't understand it," the student is commenting upon his perception of the story and his perception of himself. When a teacher says of a class, "They didn't really understand *Peter Rabbit* as an existentialist treatment of rabbithood like *Watership Down;* they just saw it as a simple kid's story," that teacher is saying that the students did not construe the text as complex and so overestimated their capacities as readers.

Those of us concerned with the formation of the literature curriculum and with the assessment of literature learning have long been concerned with the issue of difficulty. We have had to face the issue of difficulty in our determination of what is to be tested and how. In part that search has focused on the nature of textual difficulty, and how to determine the relative difficulty of one text as opposed to another. The search for an answer has extended to the question of how one determines that one student is "better" than another. Since examiners must deal with a psychometric world that seeks certainty and definitiveness of answers, reliability in the rating of performance and the ability to rank students on a "true" scale from the able reader to the insensitive clod, they face a complex set of problems. It is the purpose of this volume to seek to address this dilemma and the fundamental contradictions in the very term "examination of literary understanding."

These are the sorts of issues and the approach to the idea of difficulty that are taken up in the essays that constitute *The Idea of Difficulty in Literature.* Originally commissioned by the Center for the Learning and Teaching of Literature, a center supported by a grant from the United States Department of Education and the National Endowment for the Arts, the authors were asked to approach the concept of difficulty in literature from their own viewpoint. The authors were chosen for the diversity of their viewpoints and backgrounds, and the request was for each to shape and reconstruct the question as seemed best. What is amazing is that despite the diversity of background and approach, the authors converge upon the constructivist view. Difficulty is a social construct, often enforced by schools, rather than a simple objective property. Put in psychological terms, difficulty lives in the eye of the beholder; it may be seen as based upon beholders' estimate of the object as well as their estimate of their capacity to deal with that object in a fashion appropriate to a given situation.

We may see this in many of the statements of readers: "That's a hard book; it deals with something I don't know much about." "This book is written in a simple style; it's easy to read." "I have trouble reading books that are filled with metaphors; they make you work too hard." Such a self-estimate comes from the attempt to match one's prior knowledge to the text, and such knowledge may refer to the content and vocabulary, the structure, or the style of the text. When such estimates are held by groups, they tend to become reified and seen as conditions of the texts and not as resulting from the transaction between text and reader (Rosenblatt, 1978).

The volume includes essays from several scholarly worlds: those of literary theory, which explore difficulty of texts in the light of current thinking about literature and literary theory and knowledge; those of linguistics, which considers the various issues related to textual complexity; and those of pedagogy, which explores difficulty from the perspective of the novice and expert reader and the student in the classroom. The essays, therefore, cover a broad range of scholarly interests and perspectives, and seek to unite them within a single framework, the question of difficulty. Surprisingly, they all tend to converge on the idea that difficulty of text is not simply a matter of textual qualities but more importantly of the relationship of those qualities to the demands placed upon the reader.

In the first section, which proceeds from a basis in literary theory, Wallace Chafe explores some of the linguistic constructs that appear to define difficulty for today's readers, but he cautions us against using these constructs as absolute values of quality, an error often perpetuated by the adherents of readability formulas and "plain talk." Hazard Adams then traces the history of the idea of difficulty in literature and suggests that it is often related to the social privilege of literature and its guardians. It is also related to the problem of the topicality and allusiveness of literature, which in building upon itself demands ever-increasing knowledge upon the part of readers. William Touponce then examines the notion of difficulty as it is set forth in three recent French figures, Jacques Lacan, Jacques Derrida, and Roland Barthes. These writers have all elaborated theories of the text and related these theories to the problems of reading the text. The final author in this section, Helen Elam, turns to difficulty as a psychological and humanistic construct, and elaborates how that construct "problematizes" reading, and teases out the difficulty of reading and what is read, thus challenging the institutional practices that seek to make things simple.

In the second section, the authors begin with the institutions that can both work to make things difficult and seek to make them simple. Gunnar Hansson shows how the constraints of formal discourse about literature often serve to make the texts more difficult than they might actually be. Referring to the corpus of his research since his replication of I. A. Richards's classic study (1929), Hansson shows that problems of reading are intertwined with problems of articulating the response to what is read. Susan Hynds and Martin Nystrand each demonstrate the ways in which classrooms and teachers in the United States serve to prove Hansson's thesis. Hynds explores the questions that teachers ask and shows how they reflect codes and conventions of learning more than the nature of the text. She suggests that it is possible to change those codes and conventions. In his paper, Nystrand demonstrates the ways in which the complex of assignments, discussions, and texts can make literature study more or less difficult. In the final chapter, Purves seeks to pull many of the ideas of the other authors together to suggest a theory of the social nature of difficulty in literature and literature education, and the implications of this theory for instruction and assessment.

The volume, then, moves from theory to practice to theory, from the text to the reader and back again. All of the papers clearly support the concept of literature reading and literature learning as social events bound by the cultures of readers as well as by the cultures of the texts read. The implications for education are clear: simplistic notions of text difficulty and difficulty in learning to read, talk, and write about literature cannot withstand scrutiny, but must be replaced by notions that view the whole web of meaning and the making of meaning in our society.

REFERENCES

Richards, I. A. (1929). *Practical criticism*. New York: Harcourt Brace.

Rosenblatt, L. M. (1978). *The reader, the text, and the poem*. Carbondale: Southern Illinois University Press.

I

Difficulty in Theory and Practice

1.

Sources of Difficulty in the Processing of Written Language

Wallace Chafe

The ease with which people can process language varies considerably with the nature of the language involved. There are reasons to suppose that ordinary spoken language is the easiest kind of language to produce and understand. Linguists have been fond of pointing out that humans have been talking with each other for as long as they have been human, and that all normal people learn to talk early in their lives without any special training. As the result of a long evolutionary development, people seem to be "wired up" for the facile use of ordinary spoken language. There are less ordinary kinds of spoken language—making speeches, debating, reciting rituals—that require special preparation and talent for their production, and may also require extra effort in listening. Spoken language of these kinds can thus be regarded as more difficult.

When it comes to written language, we know that humans have been using it for only a brief, recent segment of their existence as a species. We know that facility with writing and reading come well after facility with talking and listening in an individual's development, that such skills are consciously learned and taught, and that for most people they are never practiced with the same natural ease that characterizes the use of ordinary spoken language. Given the time span of evolution, it would be absurd to think that people are wired up to use written language as such. If we wonder how they can be equipped to use it at all, perhaps the answer lies in the fact that writing takes advantage of certain other capacities that evolved in the human species for other reasons: facility with the hands, for example, and the preeminence for humans of visual information. It may be in general more difficult to process written language than spoken, but our interest here is going to be in the further question of whether there are different varieties of written language that show different degrees of processing difficulty.

The average reader would probably not hesitate to agree that some works, some authors, or some genres are harder to read than others. But what kinds of things lead people to such judgments? That is the question to be explored here. I will approach it from the point of view of a linguist whose chief interest has been in what makes writing different from speaking. My point of departure will be the belief that there are certain aspects of ordinary spoken language that enhance or retard its processibility, and that the processibility of written language can be affected by the presence or absence of analogous features. At the same time, however, I will warn against the simple conclusion that it is in all ways a good thing to "write as you speak."

READABILITY

In giving thought to such matters we can hardly ignore the fact that, since at least the 1920s, there has existed a research tradition whose goal has been to specify in quantitative terms just what it is that makes writing easy or difficult: to quantify what has been called readability. Unfortunately, these studies became mired in a certain degree of commercial success, while failing to achieve academic reputability. (Klare, 1974, provides a useful survey of such research. Other possible directions for readability research have been adumbrated, for example, in Hirsch, 1977, and Holland, 1981.) Part of the problem has been that readability is an area where research and application come together with greater impact than is usually the case. There is an obvious and demonstrated commercial, not to mention political, value in being able to say that one piece of writing is more readable than another, or that a certain book has the readability appropriate to a certain grade level. These practical benefits have encouraged the acceptance of easy-to-apply shortcuts.

A deeper aspect of the problem has been that readability, on thoughtful inspection, shows itself to be a highly complex, many-sided topic whose fuller understanding requires insights from many disciplines, perhaps even research techniques that are still not well developed. The behaviorist and structuralist biases that have dominated so much of language research during the twentieth century have simply not been up to shedding much light on a topic as intimately entwined in the complexities of human experience as this one.

On a more specific level, readability research has suffered from an inability to separate causes from effects, to distinguish between determinants of readability and ways of assessing readability itself. Thus, for example, the cloze test came to be used as a common measure of readability, in disregard of the real function of that test as a measure of redundancy. It may be true that an optimal level of redundancy makes language easier to process, all other things being equal. The effects on language processing of too little or too much redundancy would be interesting to study in detail. But redundancy is at best one of the determinants of readability, a cause rather than an effect. A test of redundancy can hardly be appropriate as a measure of readability itself.

EASE OF PROCESSING

The discussion here will not be quantitative at all, but will explore qualitatively what some of the diverse determinants of reading ease or difficulty might be, attempting to get a little closer to a fuller understanding of their complexity. To avoid the connotations of the term "readability," I will refer to "ease of processing." My major focus will be on various properties of language that may contribute to such ease. I will assume that humans are endowed genetically with certain language-processing capacities, that language most in tune with those capacities is the easiest to process, and furthermore that the language best fitting that role is ordinary speech.

Certainly, as mentioned, it would be wrong to conclude from this discussion that writing is easiest to process when it is most like ordinary spoken language. There are fundamental differences between the acts of speaking and writing. Spoken language is produced and received as evanescent sound, expressing ideas that move forward at an inexorable temporal rate. Written language is produced and received as more or less permanent visual marks, expressing ideas that may be processed at quite different rates than those of speaking or listening. Written language also creates various expectations concerning language structure and use that may be quite different from those associated with speaking. For such reasons, the approach I will follow here needs to be interpreted with caution. I believe, nevertheless, that this approach does provide useful clues. If it fails to provide complete and final answers, it does give us useful handles on various determinants of ease and difficulty.

I should mention another potential pitfall. It would be easy to conclude from this kind of discussion that language that is easier to process is "better" than language that is more difficult. Easily processible language is, of course, better with respect to that one property. But language has many dimensions, and it surely would be wrong to view ease of processing as a goal that overrides all else. For certain writers at certain times it even has been regarded as a quality to be avoided; for some, a literary work that is difficult to process may be valued for just that reason.

As a basis for discussion, I will take a small piece of writing for which there is reason to think that it is relatively difficult to read, compare it with a piece that is thought to be less difficult, and compare both samples with some things that are known about spoken language. For specific aspects of spoken and written language, I will rely especially on findings set forth

in Chafe (1982, 1986), and Chafe and Danielewicz (1987). (For a comprehensive bibliographic review of research on differences between spoken
and written language, see Chafe and Tannen, 1987.)

The writing samples are the first paragraph, or first 250 words, of
Henry James's *The Ambassadors;* and the first four paragraphs, or first 259
words, of Edith Wharton's *Ethan Frome.* These novels were both produced in the early years of this century by authors who knew and influenced each other. Nevertheless, there is reason to think that the James
passage is significantly harder to read than the Wharton. To test my own
judgment to that effect, I asked six well-read adults to read the two passages (presented in random order) and to say which of them, if either,
they found easier to read. All six agreed that the Wharton passage was
easier, two of them adding that it was *much* easier. While it would be
desirable to support this finding with more sophisticated ways of measuring relative processing ease, these responses will serve as a basis for the
discussion here. (For a discussion of the James excerpt from a partially
different perspective, see Watt, 1969.)

The James paragraph reads as follows:

Strether's first question, when he reached the hotel, was about
his friend; yet on his learning that Waymarsh was apparently not
to arrive till evening he was not wholly disconcerted. A telegram
from him bespeaking a room "only if not noisy," reply paid, was
produced for the enquirer at the office, so that the understanding they should meet at Chester rather than at Liverpool
remained to that extent sound. The same secret principle,
however, that had prompted Strether not absolutely to desire
Waymarsh's presence at the dock, that had led him thus to postpone for a few hours his enjoyment of it, now operated to make
him feel he could still wait without disappointment. They would
dine together at the worst, and, with all respect to dear old Waymarsh—if not even, for that matter, to himself—there was little
fear that in the sequel they shouldn't see enough of each other.
The principle I have just mentioned as operating had been, with
the most newly disembarked of the two men, wholly instinctive—the fruit of a sharp sense that, delightful as it would be to
find himself looking, after so much separation, into his comrade's
face, his business would be a trifle bungled should he simply
arrange for this countenance to present itself to the nearing
steamer as the first "note" of Europe. Mixed with everything
was the apprehension, already, on Strether's part, that it would,
at best, throughout, prove the note of Europe in quite a
sufficient degree.

The Wharton passage is the following:

I had the story, bit by bit, from various people, and, as generally happens in such cases, each time it was a different story.

If you know Starkfield, Massachusetts, you know the post-office. If you know the post-office you must have seen Ethan Frome drive up to it, drop the reins on his hollow-backed bay and drag himself across the brick pavement to the white colonnade: and you must have asked who he was.

It was there that, several years ago, I saw him for the first time; and the sight pulled me up sharp. Even then he was the most striking figure in Starkfield, though he was but the ruin of a man. It was not so much his great height that marked him, for the "natives" were easily singled out by their lank longitude from the stockier foreign breed: it was the careless powerful look he had, in spite of a lameness checking each step like the jerk of a chain. There was something bleak and unapproachable in his face, and he was so stiffened and grizzled that I took him for an old man and was surprised to hear that he was not more than fifty-two. I had this from Harmon Gow, who had driven the stage from Bettsbridge to Starkfield in pre-trolley days and knew the chronicle of all the families on his line.

"He's looked that way ever since he had his smash-up; and that's twenty-four years ago come next February," Harmon threw out between reminiscent pauses. I had the story, bit by bit, from various people, and, as generally happens in such cases, each time it was a different story.

DIFFERENCES OF LANGUAGE AND CULTURE

Before we turn to specific linguistic differences, we can note the effects of differences in the language or culture of the reader compared with those of the author. It is ordinarily more difficult to read a foreign language than one's own native language. A similar difficulty presents itself to a greater or lesser degree in reading works that were written at historically different stages of one's own language, or by writers who speak a dialect different from one's own. James was writing at a somewhat different time from ours, and was under the influence of British English. He used expressions such as *bespeaking a room* or *the (first) note of Europe* that to modern Americans are at least unfamiliar, as in the first case, and perhaps difficult to interpret, as in the second. He also sometimes used a kind of syntax that would not be found in either spoken or written American English at the present time, as when he wrote *had prompted Strether not absolutely to desire Waymarsh's presence.*

It is not only unfamiliar words, phrases, and locutions that may create some difficulty, but also the description of unfamiliar patterns of behavior. Thus, a contemporary American reader might expect that a hotel guest would make an inquiry *at the desk* rather than *at the office*. Although the same reader might know more or less where Liverpool is, or at least that it is a major city in England, the same cannot be said for Chester. In my own curiosity I went so far as to consult an atlas to confirm that Chester must be somewhere not too far from Liverpool. Such activities, while educational, are obvious hindrances to facile reading.

In the Wharton passage, the most obvious difference of this sort is the reference to a *hollow-backed bay*, a categorization that must have meant more to people in the preautomobile age than it does now. *Starkfield* can be accepted as a fictitious toponym, although readers familiar with the area might pause to speculate on its possible origin as a blend of Stockbridge and Pittsfield, both close to Wharton's home in the Berkshires.

Hindrances of this sort can be expected to increase with the distance between the reader's period and subculture and those of the author. They are helpful to us here in making it especially plain that ease of processing is not to be confused with literary value. Shakespeare is difficult to read for the same kinds of reasons, multiplied and magnified many times over.

INTERRUPTIONS IN INFORMATION FLOW

A promising area of linguistic research is that concerned with information flow. Central to this research is the investigation of how ideas move into and out of the consciousness of language users. In ordinary conversation ideas enter and leave the consciousness of the interactants in an easy sort of flow. Aspects of this flow are reflected in such linguistic features as the ordering of words, the use of pronouns, and the use of prosody (intonation, stresses, pauses, and the like). Processing is likely to be easier for written language that comes closer to mimicking ordinary conversation with respect to these features. (See Chafe, 1987, for a discussion of information flow in speech, and Chafe, 1988, with regard to prosodic features in written language.)

One of the most characteristic features of James's writing style is his frequent habit of interrupting ideas by inserting other ideas inside them. The paragraph we are considering includes numerous examples of such discontinuities. Among the examples quoted below, the second is particularly striking because of its two coordinate insertions, within the second of which there is still another insertion. The last two examples both show two coordinate insertions each:

Strether's first question, *when he reached the hotel*, was about his friend

and, *with all respect to dear old Waymarsh,—if not even, for that matter, to himself*—there was little fear that. . .

had been, *with the most newly disembarked of the two men*, wholly instinctive

to find himself looking, *after so much separation*, into his comrade's face

the apprehension, *already, on Strether's part*, that it would

that it would, *at best, throughout*, prove the note of Europe

Such interruptions were very popular in turn-of-the-century writing, and Edith Wharton engaged in them as well, though more sparingly:

and, *as generally happens in such cases*, each time it was a different story

it was there that, *several years ago*, I saw him for the first time

The study reported in Chafe and Danielewicz (1987) found the insertion of such phrases within phrases to be very rare in ordinary spoken language. By definition such insertions constitute interruptions in the easy flow of ideas.

PROBLEMS WITH REFERENCE

Ordinary spoken language flows most smoothly when both or all parties know who and what is being talked about. Usually, for example, there is enough shared knowledge that the use of proper names will be understood by those who are involved in a conversation.

A well-known literary device is to present people and events as if they were already familiar to the reader, as a way of pretending that the author and the reader already share some knowledge. Thus James begins by referring to *Strether* and *his friend*, who we gather must be the same person as *Waymarsh*. He treats the hotel as if we were already in a position to identify it. This pretense is so common at the beginnings of literary works that one might question whether it presents any difficulty at all. Nevertheless, it does force readers to take the cognitive step of establishing new mental "files" for people and things about whom they initially know nothing, and for whom they expect to fill in further information as the story proceeds. It contrasts with the more oral device of properly introducing new characters. To take a familiar kind of example from oral literature, to begin a story by saying *There was once a miller who was very poor, but he had a beautiful daughter* does not pretend that we already know either the miller or his daughter.

More serious problems arise when ambiguity is introduced. Problems of this nature are far from unknown in conversation. A speaker, for example, may use a personal pronoun like *he* in a context where its referent is unclear to the listener. An interested listener is able to ask for clarification by saying, *Who do you mean?*, or the like. Readers, compared with listeners, are at a disadvantage in such cases because there is no direct way to question the author. The kind of problem that may arise is well illustrated by the first part of the second sentence of the James paragraph:

A telegram from *him* bespeaking a room "only if not noisy," reply paid, was produced for *the enquirer* at the office

Readers confronting the word *him* are in a context where they have just finished processing two other third-person masculine singular pronouns. The preceding sentence ended:

yet on *his* learning that Waymarsh was apparently not to arrive till evening *he* was not wholly disconcerted.

In this context, the expected interpretation of *him* in *a telegram from him* is that its referent is identical with that of the preceding *his* and *he*—namely, the person named Strether. Since this is only the second sentence in the book, there is almost no larger context to provide help at this point. Thus, it is at first natural to suppose that Strether was the one who "bespoke" a room.

With such an interpretation in mind, the reader cannot help but be confused on reaching the words *the enquirer,* for who can this enquirer be? That he is not the same person as *him* is suggested in two ways. First, if he were the same person the reader might expect to find the word *him* in both places. Second, to the extent that events are clear at all at this point, it would not seem that the sender of the telegram and the enquirer at the office should be the same person. Readers may now try the hypothesis that, in spite of its context, *him* refers to Waymarsh and *the enquirer* to Strether. This hypothesis seems confirmed as the paragraph proceeds, but such referential gymnastics fail to contribute to ease of processing.

Later in the paragraph one encounters further referential games with *the most newly disembarked of the two men* (Strether) and *this countenance* (Waymarsh). Given what may be a muddy understanding of the situation at this point, the referents of these two phrases may require a moment's thought. The same can be said of *the principle I have just mentioned as operating*. Two long sentences before this phrase, the author introduced the idea of *the same secret principle*. The intervening complicated sentence about dining together may have consumed enough of the reader's processing capacity to suppress awareness of *the principle*. I, at least, found it necessary on first reading to go back and refresh my memory as to what the principle was. I will return below to problems with this principle.

SUBJECTS THAT EXPRESS NEW INFORMATION

My own recent work in the area of information flow has focused on the distribution of given, accessible, and new information in spoken and written language. There is no space here to present this work in detail, but one finding that can be described briefly is that nearly all the grammatical subjects in ordinary spoken language have the status of what has often been called *given* information. An idea that is given—it may be the idea of a person, object, event, or state—is one that is already active in the speaker's consciousness, and one that the speaker assumes to be already active in the listener's consciousness as well. Metaphorically, given information is already "in the air" for both the speaker and the hearer, or at least the speaker believes this to be so. Grammatical subjects function to express the starting points for adding new information, and thus it is natural that the ideas they express should strongly tend to have this given status.

Writers are free of the constraints imposed by the need to produce language on the run, as speakers must do, and are able to rework their products as much and as often as they choose. Among other effects, these freedoms often lead writers to introduce grammatical subjects that express new, rather than given, information. James provides us with some good examples. The subject of the very first sentence in *The Ambassadors* is *Strether's first question*. This phrase expresses the idea of an event that readers can in no way be assumed to have already active in their minds. It is a new idea that readers must first assimilate, before they use it as an anchor to which they can attach the further new idea that this question *was about his friend*. As mentioned earlier, however, we may be able to accept the fiction that the idea of Strether's first question was already accessible to the reader as the story began, being thus an example of knowledge pretended to be shared between the author and the reader.

The same can hardly be said of the subject of the second sentence: *A telegram from him bespeaking a room "only if not noisy," reply paid*. This long, information-packed subject imposes on the reader a cluster of new ideas, all centered on the idea of the telegram. It does not refer to anything already given or accessible, even in pretense, but rather moves the story forward in a significant way. The author does not pretend that we already know of the telegram, as is shown quite clearly by his use of the indefinite article: a telegram. This is a grammatical subject that not only bears new information, but expresses a complex set of new ideas.

The same sentence ends with a result clause introduced by *so that.* The subject of this clause is equally filled with new and complex information: *the understanding they should meet at Chester rather than at Liverpool.* The prize for newness and complexity, however, goes to the subject of the third sentence: *The same secret principle, however, that had prompted Strether not absolutely to desire Waymarsh's presence at the dock, that had led him thus to postpone for a few hours his enjoyment of it.*

These subjects packed with new information contrast markedly with the given-information subjects expressed by pronouns at the beginning of the Wharton passage:

I had the story

it was a different story

If *you* know Starkfield

you know the post-office

The *it* in the second Wharton example is a typical, pronominalized, given subject, referring to the idea of the story that was activated as new information in the third and fourth words of the novel. As for the other examples, in spoken language first- and second-person pronouns have the status of given information because of the inherent makeup of a conversation: the participants are already conscious of each others' existence and identity. Some writers pretend that the same situation exists between themselves and their readers; hence the naturalness and ease of the *I* and *you* in the other Wharton examples.

NEGATION

One other hindrance to information flow is worth passing mention. A noticeable property of the James passage is its frequent use of negation, manifested especially in the word *not,* but also in negative words such as *disconcerted* and *without:*

yet on his learning that Waymarsh was apparently *not* to arrive till evening he was *not* wholly *disconcerted*

bespeaking a room "only if *not* noisy"

that had prompted Strether *not* absolutely to desire Waymarsh's presence at the dock

he could still wait *without* disappointment

if *not* even, for that matter, to himself

they should*n't* see enough of each other

Negative expressions must be understood against a background in which the reader would have expected the opposite. Thus, I would not say *I didn't go the movie last night* unless I had reason to believe that you expected me to have gone to the movie. On reading a negative clause, therefore, a reader is forced to take the extra step of imagining that the opposite was expected: that Waymarsh *would* have arrived before evening, that Strether *would* have been disconcerted, and so on. The mental act of constructing these expectations and then negating them qualifies as another hindrance to ease of processing. The problem increases when the reader needs to process the kind of double negation conveyed in a phrase like *not wholly disconcerted*.

INVOLVEMENT AND DETACHMENT

A listener's or reader's interest in a piece of language is heightened by the presence of features that have sometimes been grouped under the term "evaluation" (Labov, 1972: 354–96) and sometimes called "involvement" (Chafe, 1982; Tannen, 1989). These are linguistic devices whose effect is to cause a listener or reader to feel caught up in the ideas and events being verbalized, to experience something akin to what the writer was experiencing. Wharton, for example, increases the reader's involvement, not only by telling her story in the first person, but even by addressing her reader in the second: *If you know Starkfield, Massachusetts, you know the post-office.* The same segment illustrates the use of repetition, one of the major involvement devices treated by Tannen (in press): *you know* is stated three times, and *you must have*, twice. The alliteration in the phrase *lank longitude* illustrates another kind of repetition. Wharton adds to feelings of involvement with her vivid descriptions of events and persons: *drag himself across the brick pavement, the sight pulled me up sharp, the most striking figure in Starkfield, a lameness checking each step like the jerk of a chain, bleak and unapproachable, stiffened and grizzled.*

The most exciting event, in fact the only event, in the James paragraph is the fact that somebody produced a telegram for the enquirer. This event is reported in the passive voice so that the producer of the telegram can be left unidentified. The passive is relatively rare in ordinary spoken language, outside lexicalized phrases like *I got hit.* By shifting attention away from an agent doing something to an object having something done to it, the passive is one of the prime manifestations of detachment, or negative involvement.

Another manifestation of detachment is the use of nominalizations: nouns formed from verbs or adjectives. Nominalizations are used with great frequency in more detached styles of writing, and are not present to anything like the same degree in ordinary conversation. The James paragraph contains the following examples: *learning, enquirer, understanding, presence, enjoyment, disappointment, separation,* and *apprehension.* Nominalizations reify events and properties, converting what are initially experienced as dynamic, short-lived happenings and feelings into ideas that have the same static, lasting quality as the ideas of physical objects. Thus, instead of saying that Waymarsh *understood* that they should meet at Chester rather than at Liverpool, James wrote about Waymarsh's *understanding* as if it were a thing, something that could then acquire lasting properties such as being sound. By using nominalizations so frequently, James repeatedly forces readers to abstract away from ordinary experience.

Wharton's use of *sight, lameness, smash-up,* and *pause* adds up to only half the number of nominalizations used by James. Wharton also uses such words in close association with active verbs, thereby moderating their contribution to detachment: *I saw him . . . the sight; a lameness checking each step.*

Paragraphing

It is not irrelevant that the two pieces of writing before us show markedly different divisions into paragraphs. The James selection consists of 250 words, or six sentences, embraced within a single paragraph. The 259 words or nine sentences of the Wharton selection are distributed among four paragraphs. Looking a little beyond these selections we find that the first eight paragraphs of James's novel have a mean length of nine sentences, while Wharton's first eight paragraphs have a mean length of two and a half sentences. (The reason is not entirely that Wharton includes some dialogue, since James also includes reported speech within his paragraphs.)

Writing styles vary greatly in their preference for paragraph size. The minimum paragraph can be found on the front page of nearly any newspaper, where the mean number of sentences per paragraph is only a little more than one. The maximum I have found has been in certain writings in the *New Yorker,* where paragraphs containing several dozen sentences are not unusual.

Intuition suggests that a correlation between paragraph size and ease of processing would repay further study. As William Zinsser put it, "Short paragraphs put air around what you write and make it look inviting, whereas one long chunk of type can discourage the reader from even starting to read" (Zinsser, 1980: 111–12). Ultimately we would like to understand why this is so. My work with spoken language suggests that speech does exhibit paragraphlike units, the boundaries of which are signaled by increased hesitating and a falling off of pitch and volume, followed by a new burst of energy (Lehiste, 1979). These boundaries are associated with significant changes of scene, time, character configuration, event structure, or in general with some kind of topical discontinuity (Chafe 1980: 40–47; 1987: 42–45). To put it in other terms, paragraphlike boundaries appear in speech when the speaker replaces one set of background concepts, held in peripheral memory, with another. When a writer, like James or one of the *New Yorker* authors (or editors), favors us with long paragraphs, he is suggesting that we are able to hold a fairly large amount of background information in our minds at once. The front page of the newspaper assumes that our capacity for retaining background information is much more limited.

There is more to notice about paragraphs than their length. Traditionally, instruction in writing has had much to say about paragraph "structure," with a supposition that the organization and coherence of paragraphs can also influence ease of processing, positively or negatively. In this connection I can mention Rodgers's (1966) study of Walter Pater's paragraphing in his essay called "Style" (Pater, 1987). Pater's practice is interesting because he was very conscious of what he was doing in this respect. Rodgers shows that Pater's reasons for distributing his ideas among paragraphs were diverse and complex. Logic and coherence played a role, but were by no means the only determining factors: "the logical partitioning of complex discourse into paragraphs can occur at so many junctures that additional nonlogical criteria often have to be invoked to account for a given decision to indent" (Rodgers, 1966: 11). Nonlogical criteria may include reader expectation, paragraph size, readability, rhythm, parallelisms, juxtapositions, and "tonal fluctuations." Rodgers's study may be unique in showing how diverse the grounds for paragraphing can be, as exemplified by an author who prided himself on how well he did it.

This brings us, then, to the question of how information flow may be helped or hindered by the clarity with which ideas are presented, and the complexity with which they are related. At one extreme, ideas may be presented in a straightforward, obvious way, where each is clear in itself and where the relation of each to the others is made equally clear as the text proceeds. The Wharton passage is of this nature. One need not work very hard at understanding each idea as it appears, or at relating one idea to the next.

James requires more effort of this kind. Take, for example, *the secret principle* that is introduced in the third sentence, and that might be said to be the topic of this paragraph. From the third sentence we learn, not what that principle was, but that it *had prompted Strether not absolutely to desire Waymarsh's presence at the dock.* Next we learn that it *operated to make him feel he could still wait without disappointment.* Finally, toward the end of the paragraph, we learn that Strether has an apprehension that his upcoming contact with Waymarsh will *prove the note of Europe in quite a sufficient degree.* We gather that the secret principle is one that works to postpone contact between Strether and Waymarsh, while making Strether apprehensive about the length and frequency of such contact. We are left wondering about the reasons for Strether's apprehension, and of course that wonderment is what makes us want to read on.

Something more subtle occurs later in the logic of this paragraph. My first reading gave me the sense that the author was confused or confusing when he wrote of arranging for *this countenance to present itself to the nearing steamer.* I understood from the early part of the paragraph that Strether had already landed (at Liverpool?) and gone to the hotel (at Chester?). Why then should the author now be writing about what would happen when Strether landed? I reckoned without the force of the words *had been* in the clause *the principle I have just mentioned as operating had been . . . wholly instinctive.* The effect of these two words was to throw the rest of this sentence into a pluperfect time, before the events described earlier in the paragraph: a time when Strether was still aboard the ship. This subtlety of tense manipulation requires not only careful reading, but also the option of looking back to refresh one's perception of just how things had been worded. Readers can do this in a way that listeners cannot, but it constitutes still another hindrance to ease of processing.

VALUES

The need for careful reading, including the option of rereading, is in fact a primary value of the James style of writing, a value that removes it from any close resemblance to ordinary spoken language, and by the same token from facile processing—a value that makes it "difficult." Authors like James must have viewed literature as sharing qualities of a painting or sculpture whose meaning cannot be fully appreciated at first glance, but must be savored slowly as one looks and relooks and thinks and rethinks about what the artist has done. Leon Edel concludes his introduction to the novel with the following observation:

> There are readers for whom certain books will always remain closed; and others for whom the same books cannot be opened

too often. James wrote *The Ambassadors* for the attentive reader, and a reader capable of *seeing* with him—and accepting his painter-sense, his brush-work, his devotion to picture and to scene and above all his need to render this in a highly colored and elaborate style, so as to capture the nuances of his perceptions. The reader who is able to give him "attention of perusal," will discover soon enough the particular rewards of this book. (James, 1960: xv–xvi)

In avoiding the pitfall of thinking that when writing is easier to process it is for that reason "better," we should not let James lead us into the opposite trap of supposing that the value of writing necessarily increases with its difficulty. Writing serves many purposes, the more practical of which are surely advanced by ease of processing. For instructions or legal documents there are very practical reasons for preferring readability. But literature has other functions, and whether ease or difficulty is to be preferred aesthetically is impossible to answer. The ingredients of beauty are many, and changeable with time, place, and the eye of the beholder. To make things easy for one's readers or to make them hard are both strategies that can be exploited with good or bad results. In short, it would be clearly wrong to associate any absolute scale of value with the features I have discussed here.

REFERENCES

Chafe, W. (1980). "The deployment of consciousness in the production of a narrative." In W. Chafe, ed., *The pear stories: Cognitive, cultural, and linguistic aspects of narrative production*. Norwood, N.J.: Ablex.

———. (1982). "Integration and involvement in speaking, writing, and oral literature." In D. Tannen, ed., *Spoken and written language: Exploring orality and literacy*. Norwood, N.J.: Ablex.

———. (1986). "Writing in the perspective of speaking." In C. Cooper and S. Greenbaum, eds., *Studying writing: Linguistic approaches. Written Communication Annual, vol. 1*. Beverly Hills: Sage.

———. (1987). "Cognitive constraints on information flow." In R. Tomlin, ed., *Coherence and grounding in discourse*. Amsterdam: John Benjamins.

———. (1988). "Punctuation and the prosody of written language." *Written Communication*, 5, 395–426.

Chafe, W., and Danielewicz, J. (1987). "Properties of spoken and written language." In R. Horowitz and S. J. Samuels, eds., *Comprehending oral and written language*. New York: Academic Press.

Chafe, W., and Tannen, D. (1987). "The relation between written and spoken language." *Annual Review of Anthropology*, 16, 383–407.

Hirsch, E. D., Jr. (1977). *The philosophy of composition*. Chicago: University of Chicago Press.

Holland, V. M. (1981). *Psycholinguistic alternatives to readability formulas*. Document Design Project, Technical Report no. 12. Washington, D.C.

James, H. (1960). *The ambassadors*. Leon Edel, ed. New York: Houghton Mifflin (originally published 1903).

Klare, G. B. (1974). "Assessing readability." *Reading Research Quarterly*, 10, 62–102.

Labov, W. (1972). *Language in the inner city: Studies in the Black English vernacular*. Philadelphia: University of Pennsylvania Press.

Lehiste, I. (1979). "Sentence boundaries and paragraph boundaries— perceptual evidence." In R. Clyne, W. F. Hanks, and C. L. Hofbauer, eds., *The elements: A parasession on linguistic units and levels*. Chicago Linguistic Society. University of Chicago.

Pater, W. (1987). *Appreciations: With an essay on style*. Evanston: Northwestern University Press (originally published 1889).

Rodgers, C., Jr. (1966). "A discourse-centered rhetoric of the paragraph." *College Composition and Communication*, 16, 2–11.

Tannen, D. (1989). *Talking voices: Repetition, dialogue, and imagry in conversation*. Cambridge: Cambridge University Press.

Watt, I. (1969). "The first paragraph of *The Ambassadors:* An explication." In G. A. Love and M. Payne, eds., *Contemporary essays on style: Rhetoric, linguistics, and criticism*. Glenview, Ill.: Scott, Foresman.

Wharton, E. (1911). *Ethan Frome*. New York: Charles Scribner's Sons.

Zinsser, W. (1980). *On writing well: An informal guide to writing nonfiction*. New York: Harper and Row.

2.

The Difficulty of Difficulty

Hazard Adams

The notion of literature's difficulty must have begun with the first interpreter and been early sustained by the first priesthood to have developed a vested interest in mystery. As formal interpretation in Western culture begins with commentary on Homer and holy scripture, so, no doubt, does the concept of literary difficulty. But what is deemed difficult in one age is often not what is focused on as difficult in another. In modernism and postmodernism difficulty has been perceived in new ways that challenge earlier assumptions of, among other things, the linguistic stability upon which early notions of difficulty had been based. Before we examine the implications of this for pedagogy, it is worthwhile to study some of the history of interpretation and some of the things that were (and sometimes still are) regarded as the major sources of difficulty for readers.

I.

Certainly for a long time this issue revolved around a difference between so-called literal and allegorical readings of the Bible and of classical texts. The essence of literality in this early sense is to suppose that what one is reading is a historical account. There is also often assumed to be a fictive literality or what some think of when they refer to a "good story." Yet even those who have insisted on the strict historical literality of the New Testament have interpreted Jesus' parables in an allegorical fashion; and, faced with defending "good stories" against the charge of triviality, readers have over centuries developed complex interpretations that have frequently been based on the assumption that there is in the text more than meets the eye, an allegorical depth containing a valuable precept.

I hope it is fair to say, then, that the concept of literary difficulty arose from a twofold root: first, the establishment of mystery in a holy text to be guarded and regulated by a special class of priestly initiates and, second, the desire to defend by recourse to hidden meaning secular works of fiction against those who would identify fictions with untruth. Both cases generated interpretations and interpretive traditions that gave rise to charges of willful obscurantism and outrageous liberties taken with texts. Such charges are by no means unknown today, though now based on other grounds. Generally in such interpretations the effort was to show that the text hid beneath its "literal" surface a valuable teaching, often rescuing a surface that was politically or morally suspect. The earliest readings of Homer were interpreted in the direction of what was later called moral allegory, often of a Platonic sort. Biblical readings sometimes allegorized scripture into moral precept or, in the most radical cases, doctrines in opposition to established theology, as in the Gnostic writings. Occult readings, of which Gnostic ones are some of the earliest known to us, have had sporadic popularity, often with the distinct implication that such texts are either for an elite readership or represent the essence of a tradition of spiritual truth under threat of extinction by modern materialism and science, and therefore gone underground. I shall discuss both these views, the first at some length, the second briefly, before getting down to a consideration of contemporary difficulty and the difficulty with it.

The first of these views and to some extent the second are exemplified by an essay of 1632 called "Mythomystes" by a little known writer, Henry Reynolds. He intended to defend the "ancients" against the "moderns," joining a popular critical debate of the time. In his essay he soon identifies the ancients with allegorical expression of hidden occult wisdom. Further, he distinguishes two classes of readers: a priesthood or an intelligentsia, and the unworthy vulgar or the multitude. He implies that texts of any value have usually two readings:

> It was enough for the multitude to be by merely the simple story, taught and made to know, now the power of God, now his wrath against the wicked, clemency toward the good, and justice to all; and by divine and wholesome precepts instructed in the ways of religion, and holy life. But those secreter mystics, and abstrusities of most high divinity, hidden and concealed under the bark and rude cover of the words, to have divulged and laid these open to the vulgar; what had it been other than to give holy things to dogs, and cast pearls among swine. [Reynolds, 1632/1971: 204]

Having entered the quarrel of the ancients and moderns on the side of the ancients and having invoked allegorical wisdom in their favor, Reynolds subscribes to the theory of the growing decrepitude of the world. The formerly noble estate of poetry is now abused by unlearned charlatans who are interested only in superficial delights. In its essence poetry is the conveyor of occult wisdom, which turns out to be mainly Neoplatonic doctrine—"the understanding of things even farthest removed from us, and most worthy of our speculation, and knowledge" (p. 198). But modern poets have lost touch with the substance of their predecessors' works and have copied only their "style, phrase, and manner of expression" (p. 198).

Reynolds compares the moderns to the ancients in three respects and finds them wanting in all three. First, they lack both the ancients' desire to search for high truths and their contempt for worldly profit. Second, they do not hold learning in great respect and, playing to vulgar tastes, do not (as did the ancients) conceal high truth from vulgarization. Reynolds holds that the ancients all the way back to the Egyptians "devised, to the end to retain among themselves what they had found (lest it should be abused and vilified by being delivered to the vulgar), certain marks, and characters of things, under which all the precepts of their wisdom were contained; which marks they called hieroglyphics or sacred engravings" (p. 201). Third, the moderns fail in their ignorance of the "mysteries and hidden properties of nature" (p. 204). The most learned of the ancients were the poets, who knew nature better than any others and put their knowledge into their works. Too often translators and interpreters have lost the meaning of the great poets and reduced them to moralists only. For Reynolds, knowledge of nature appears to be cabalistic science, natural magic, astrology, medicine, and physics. Those fables now regarded as scandalous are really allegories. For example:

> Who can make that rape of Proserpine, whom her mother Ceres (that under the species of corn might include as well the whole genus of the vegetable nature) sought so long for in the earth, to mean other, than the putrefaction, and succeeding generation of the seeds we commit to Pluto or the earth? . . . Or what can Jupiter's blasting of his beloved Semele, after his having deflowered her, and the wrapping of his son he got on her (Bacchus, or wine) in his thigh after his production, mean other than the necessity of the air's heat to his birth, in the generation; and (after a violent pressure and delaceration of his mother the grape) the like close imprisoning of him also, in a fit vessel, till he gain his full maturity, and come to be fit aliment? [p. 207]

It is clear enough that Reynolds is committed to a concept of poetry as rigidly allegorical. Such reservations as Francis Bacon had about allegory (and he found no small number of poems to contain it) Reynolds vehemently attacks. Bacon had confessed that he believed many interpreters had twisted ancient fables to desired meanings or turned them into philosophical statements of one school or another. This is too much for Reynolds, who finds value only in the allegorical meaning a work preserves, hides, and yet passes on. Presumably an allegorical interpretation is equivalent to the poem in every way that is important. One finds this attitude, expressed with varying vehemence, throughout the tradition in which Reynolds works.

The idea of a kind of poetic whole does, however, occur in some allegorists, who, as the early nineteenth-century Platonist Thomas Taylor suspected of Porphyry, would like to find a continuous allegory in a work rather than small allegories connected by delightful but superficial intervals. In a long footnote to his paraphrase of Porphyry's essay on the cave of the nymphs in the *Odyssey*, Taylor, for example, attempts to supply the lost unified allegorical reading of the whole *Odyssey*. Ulysses is "the image of a man passing in a regular manner from a sensible life, and advancing from darkness to light," and all events are interpreted in terms of a pattern that delivers the hero, purified in the end, to the soul and celestial love—namely, Penelope (Raine and Harper, 1969: 322–42).

Reynolds, who wanted to square his respect for ancient pagan wisdom with his Christianity, or, more probably, his Christian readership, has recourse to a concept of Greek myth as a version of biblical truth, the characters of Greek myth being made to correspond with those of the Old Testament. This bold connection of scripture and Greek myth has its counterpart in the similar allegorical methods applied to both. The allegorical interpretation of scripture has a long history, which appears in its beginnings to be tied up with an effort to eradicate anthropomorphism. As far back as *The Letter of Aristeas* (c. 100–150 B.C.) there is an allegorization of the Torah.

The connection between Neoplatonic and scriptural allegorizing is evident in Philo Judaeus (c. 50 A.D.) and in one of Porphyry's teachers, Origen (c. 185–259). Philo regarded allegorical interpretation as a method that had to be learned. One became a sort of initiate. Not always denying the literal level, he thought of it more or less as the body of thought, while the meaning revealed allegorically was the soul or was approximate to it. There is at the bottom of Philo's attitude the idea that reality as such cannot be spoken but only approximated by allegoric presentation: metaphysical fact eludes literal presentation, and the allegoric is merely the best we can achieve. Our thoughts always surpass our expression, but this should not prevent us from doing as well as we can:

> No one, whether poet or historian, could ever give expression in
> an adequate manner to the beauty of his ideas respecting the
> creation of the world; for they surpass all the power of language,
> and amaze our hearing, being too great and venerable to be

adapted to the senses of any created being. That, however, is not a reason for our yielding to indolence on the subject, but rather from our affection for the Deity we ought to endeavour to exert ourselves even beyond our powers in describing them. [Glatzer, 1971: 1]

The act of interpretation is a form of piety and celebration, and if it goes only a certain distance, that act in its very smallness affirms the greatness of the divine object, which has no name, names being "symbols [allegories] of created things; seek them not for Him who is uncreated" (Bigg, 1968: 40). Language, matter, everything but pure thought is apart from the One (Goodenough, 1962: 103).

Philo vigorously combated those who opposed allegorization. In Philo, according to S. G. Sowers:

The literal meaning corresponds to the sensible everyday world of phenomena and deals with objects, persons, events, and things of the objective world in general. On the other hand, the allegorical meaning lying beyond the literal treats of timeless ideas such as the structure of the creation, the ethical life, and the soul's journey from corporeality to incorporeality. [1965: 31]

Thus the story of Abraham is literally the history of a righteous patriarch, but on the allegorical level it is the history of a soul that turns to a higher spiritual reality. Philo's interpretations are often multiple, as in his complex treatment of Jacob's ladder, and he regards scripture as the creation of prophets who came under divine guidance and often, like Plato's possessed poets, may not have understood what they were recording. Even the interpreter must be possessed of grace to achieve the correct reading.

Jean Daniélou (1960) describes an interpretation that Philo makes of Genesis in which Adam is the understanding, Eve sensation, and the serpent pleasure. Paradise means virtue and "is planted in the East, for virtue never sleeps, nor does it cease: as the rising sun fills all darkness with light, so when virtue arises in the soul, it enlightens its night and dispels its darkness" (p. 59). Paradise is also wisdom, its trees the various virtues—an allegorization, Daniélou remarks, that is taken up by the Christian ascetic tradition. The creation of Eve is the birth of sensation, and occurs while Adam is asleep because "it is just when the spirit is asleep that sensation is most active.... The proof of this is that when we wish to think we flee into solitude, shutting our eyes, closing our ears, and shutting out the senses" (p. 60). One detects here the allegorist working very hard to justify every detail of a text in terms of a preconceived philosophy, in this case fundamentally Platonic. The tendency of this brand of scriptural interpretation is to return over and over again to certain fundamental abstract ideas, and this return in itself must have had a powerful effect on readers' ways of interpreting.

Similarly with Origen, the Genesis story is given moral meaning:

> Our interior man is composed of soul and spirit. The spirit is called man, the soul (*anima*) is called woman. If there is harmony between them they unite frequently and beget sons which are good dispositions and salutary thoughts, by which they fill the earth, that is they lead their bodily senses to higher levels. [p. 62]

There is always the problem of why God allowed the Bible to be presented to humankind in ways that render it so difficult to understand. Philo's answer to this is to attack the anthropomorphic tendency of a purely literal reading. The Bible nevertheless condescends to slow-witted, unintelligent people, who will find it difficult to conceive of God except in human terms like wrath. In any case, for Christian allegorists like Clement and Origen the principle of allegorical reading had the precedent of St. Paul's treatment of Hagar and Sarah and his statement in 2 Corinthians iii that the spirit gives life and the letter kills (Chadwick, 1966: 74). For Origen, who finds three levels of allegory—the literal (sometimes absent), the moral, and the spiritual—in scripture, an allegory is really sanctioned by its correspondence to the preconceived Platonic notion of the universe itself, where the divine wisdom is distorted and weighted down in the realm of matter. The Pauline tripartite body, soul, and spirit are thought to be reflected by analogy in this threefold scheme.

In the Reformation, allegorical interpretation was denounced by Lutherans and Calvinists, but these same people could not, of course, eradicate allegorization from their own readings. But Calvin clearly enough saw the dangers of such readings as undermining the literal factuality of scripture and called them a contrivance of Satan.

There has been among some theologians a long effort to maintain a hard and fast distinction between allegorical and typological interpretation. The basic principle of biblical typology is that the imperfect order of the Old Testament prefigures the completed order of the New, Christ fulfilling the expectations of the Old. Past events of the Old Testament are figures or types fulfilled in the New and prophetic of last things, and the figurally related events are antitypes of each other. Related to this is the concept of analogy, in which the fallen or lower realm of nature is a parallel-opposite of the higher realm, hell, and its contents being inverse counterparts of paradise and its contents.

St. Iranaeus, who attacked the Gnostics, argued that a clear eschatological order in history, demonstrated by a typological reading of the

Bible, showed God's signature upon his works. This, he claimed in a round of circular reasoning, proves the authenticity of scripture. The historical order is judged divine apparently because it has unity. Certain traditional aesthetic ideas of harmony would seem to have been applied here directly to history. For Iranaeus, the Old Testament contained four fundamental types: the ark of Noah, the crossing of the Red Sea, the Mosaic law, and the entry into the promised land. Working out a complex set of relationships to the New Testament, Iranaeus went so far as to argue that because Jesus died on a Friday, so must have his antitype Adam. The inference is that everything has its antitype. Antitypes, furthermore, can be parallels or parallel-opposites, as in this free-ranging passage from St. Ambrose in the fourth century:

> Adam is born of the virgin earth, Christ is born of a Virgin. The former was made in the image of God, the latter is the image of God. The first was set over irrational animals, the second over all living beings. By a woman came foolishness, and by a Virgin true Wisdom. A tree brought death, life comes from the Cross. While one is deprived of his spiritual endowments and is clothed with leaves, the other, deprived of earthly goods, does not regret being clothed with a body. [Daniélou, 1960: 46]

Daniélou himself displays a traditional anxious desire to maintain the historicality of events, the essence of typology being to show that history itself is figurative rather than to replace history with allegorical wisdom.

> It would be an entire abuse of language to include moral allegory with typology under the one heading of the spiritual sense, as opposed to the literal sense. Typology is a legitimate extension of the literal sense, while moral allegory is something entirely alien: the former is in truth exegesis, the latter is not. [p. 64]

But threads of allegorization run through the early typological interpretations, as in the appearance of a mystical sense, seven generations before Noah. Noah's going into the sea is, incidentally, a type of baptism, both figuring the descent to battle Leviathan, which in turn is related to Christ's descent into Hell.

No church father would claim to have discovered the principle of typology. It was regarded as implicit in the messianic writings of the Old Testament prophets, who, it is claimed, actually saw the events of their day as types to be fulfilled. It can be said without doubt, however, that the typological interpretation of events began with the very earliest Christians, even with St. Paul (Auerbach, 1959: 51–53).

The anxiety about allegory is anxiety that desires to preserve the

Bible's figural or typological historicality or literality. Daniélou argues that allegory does not represent the sense of scripture at all. It is merely the presentation of philosophy and morality under biblical imagery, the method being analogous to the Stoic presentation of morality under Homeric imagery. Typology, on the other hand, is a legitimate extension of the literal sense of the Bible.

The strict separation of the two sought by Daniélou was clouded from Origen to the Reformation, at least. One finds a nineteenth-century theologian beginning his book with an account of the mixing of the two modes, with the sole purpose of preserving historicality. Patrick Fairbairn divides allegory into two sorts:

> 1. When the scriptural representation is actually held to have had no foundation in fact—to be a mere myth, or fabulous description, invented for the sole purpose of exhibiting the mysteries of divine truth; or, 2. When the representation, even if wearing the appearance of a real transaction, is considered incapable as it stands of yielding any adequate or satisfactory sense, and is consequently employed, precisely as if it had been fabulous, to convey some meaning of a quite diverse and higher kind. [1852: 2]

The difference between a "type" and allegory of the first sense is that the type always required "the reality of the facts or circumstances stated in the original narrative" (p. 3). This is somewhat curiously put, since the facts are said to be "created" in the narrative, whereas one would suppose Fairbairn thought that the facts are faithfully recorded in it. But we shall have to let the interesting implications of this pass. The difference between a "type" and allegory of the second sense is that the typical sense is not a different or higher sense but a "different or higher application of the same sense" (p. 3). Fairbairn regards the early church fathers as much given to the second sort of allegory and explains this by imagining that, though they stuck to the Bible's historical veracity, they regarded parts of it to be at the literal level "so meagre and puerile, that it was chiefly to be regarded as the vehicle of a much more refined and ethereal instruction" (p. 3). Origen is said to have gone farther and denied the real existence of many things in the Old Testament, often arguing for a "concoction of mysteries" rather than history. Like Daniélou a century later, Fairbairn regards biblical allegorizing as a "vicious system of interpretation" (p. 3).

There can be some sympathy with this view, for the lengths to which Origen carried the method, to say nothing of his followers, is extreme. The example of Origen's interpretation of Abraham's marriage to Keturah will suffice. Origen gives an elaborate reading of this to mean that

Abraham on the death of Sarah, who is the "perfecting of virtue," must continue to be employed in learning:

> —which learning is called by the divine word his wife. Abraham, therefore, when an old man, and his body in a manner dead, took Keturah to wife. I think it was better, according to the exposition we follow, that the wife should have been received when his body was dead, and his members were mortified. For we have a greater capacity for wisdom when we hear about the dying Christ in our mortal body. Then Keturah, whom he married in his old age, is by interpretation incense, or sweet odor. For he said, even as Paul said, 'We are a sweet savor of Christ.' Sin is a foul and putrid thing; but if any of you in whom this no longer dwells, have the fragrance of righteousness, the sweetness of mercy, and by prayer continually offer up incense to God, ye also have taken Keturah to wife. [p. 4]

Whether or not this interpretation seems plausible to the reader on the face of it, it is worthwhile recalling that the whole matter gets very short shrift in the Bible. Genesis 25 has only the most brief mention of Abraham's marriage to Keturah, indicating that he had six children by her. The only other reference to her occurs in 1 Chronicles 1:32, where Keturah is called Abraham's concubine and her sons by him are listed.

The question arises whether it is possible to make a distinction between an allegorical interpretation and a meditation or building of thought upon a text, which is what Origen's interpretation above seems to be. Certainly countless sermons on biblical texts, some greatly admired, have sinned allegorically if we cannot do so. That, in turn, raises the question of whether criticism, by which throughout I simply mean intelligent reading, is or is not really always a meditation or building of thought rather than a process of extracting an allegedly indwelling meaning. Though we may if we are good postmodernists think Origen was doing the former, it is likely that he thought he was doing the latter. Whatever the case, it was practices like these that established the critical paradigm eventually applied to secular texts.

The second view mentioned above, that literary texts preserve spiritual truth against its threatened extinction in modern life, is perhaps best exemplified in the interpretive work of Kathleen Raine, whose Neoplatonic reading of William Blake and commitment to the "perennial philosophy" implies that the most important line of poetry is that which maintains the tradition of secret wisdom and protects it against the modern appropriation of truth by science (Raine, 1968).

It is fair to say that the late nineteenth century saw an upsurgence of fantastical learning in the form of literary occultism and that Raine is one heir to it. Some years ago Northrop Frye suggested that writers' embrace of occultism in the nineteenth century was more a literary phenomenon than an occult one, an attempt to hang on to a system of literary conventions in the face of the antiliterary hegemony of materialist science (Frye, 1963: 220–21). He was thinking especially, I presume, of the French symbolists' interest in the occult and esoteric, eventuating in the style of Stéphane Mallarmé, who could be said to have secularized with much irony a religious tradition of priestly occult obscurity. Charles Baudelaire had already secularized the occult doctrine of correspondences systematized for religious purposes by Emmanuel Swedenborg and had attacked materialistic literary efforts to imitate nature.

One notes that even with Reynolds and some of the churchmen, for whom the real value of a text is not what the vulgar get out of it, there is an allegorical level that will teach the multitude without corrupting the hidden truth. Even there, the appropriate reading is not the literal level, which Reynolds tends to disregard. The dangers are not those that the biblical typologist has worried about but those that any teacher of literature encounters in the inexperienced student who is suddenly exposed to allegorical reading and proceeds freestyle to achieve an outlandishness that would have given even Origen pause. Such was my student who thought Blake's "The Sick Rose" really to be about a kind of plant disease he had learned of in his agriculture class. Or is this an excess of a certain literality? Perhaps it is best to describe it as the misplacement of a paradigm or the lack of a literary one. It is also bringing one's subjective experience to bear with innocent vengeance.

Is there, once history is dismissed and we are in the area of fiction, a literal level that can be read in an unproblematic way? I doubt it, just as postmodernism tends to doubt it. The doubt may be proved by another student who began a paper for me on "Ode on a Grecian Urn" with the sentence, "John Keats went up into his attic and found this old shape." This was years before anyone in America had heard of deconstruction, but the sentence certainly problematizes the literal rendering of Keats's phrase "O Attic shape." Or is it that the student took too doggedly the teacher's admonition to consider poems to be little dramas and had to locate Keats somewhere—in the attic?

The medieval fourfold tradition of interpretation formalized by John Cassian and St. Thomas Aquinas with respect to scripture and later secularized by Dante Alighieri proposes a "literal" level and identifies it with the historical. It then adds the "spiritual" level, which it divides into three parts—the "allegorical" (in a narrower sense than I have been using the term, since all three are types of allegory in the broader sense), the "moral," and the "anagogic." One proceeds up this scale to readings containing more and more exalted spiritual truth. St. Thomas (1256–72/1971) wrote:

Whereas in every other science things are signified by words, this science has the property that the things signified by the words have themselves also a signification. Therefore that first signification whereby words signify things belongs to the first sense, the historical or literal. That signification whereby things signified by words have themselves also a signification is called the spiritual sense, which is based on the literal, and presupposes it. [pp. 118–19]

So to those who would interpret scripture, "literal" means historical, and in many theological quarters there was (and still is), as I have pointed out, considerable suspicion of allegorical interpretation because of the fear that it would spirit away the historicality of the Bible. For St. Thomas the "allegorical" level of the text was what we and earlier ages call the typological, in which the old law is a figure of the new law. This did not interfere with the truth of history, for it was regarded as definitely historical. So too with the "anagogical," since that referred to the end of history, the new law being in turn a "figure of future glory." St. Thomas connects the "moral" sense to Christ and relates it, therefore, to what he regarded as the meaning of historical fact. It was the platonizing kind of allegory mentioned above that threatened biblical history, since one read quickly through the literal to ascertain its arcane meaning.

Such meanings are not likely to be reached by very many readers unless they have been trained in typological method. There is no question that the authors of the New Testament were themselves typologists and that the New and Old Testaments are full of analogies to each other. However, the ingenuity of some of the later typological readings exceeds anything they were likely to have put there and would never have been exercised as it was without some traditional endorsement of the method and a certain attitude establishing its powers and limits. The method was accomplished by assumptions that a "moral sense" was totally consistent with a typological, historical reading of scripture. It is not surprising that as a secular criticism took shape in medieval times there was a tendency to think of the reading of at least some secular texts in terms inherited from the theologians.

The most famous explicit secularization of the Thomistic fourfold method was that of Dante. It appears in two places, first in the *Convito* and then (though the authorship is disputed) in a 1318 letter to Can Grande della Scala. But, of course, for Dante the literal level did not have to be historical with the urgency felt by those who needed to preserve the Bible's historical truth. In his secularization Dante points out that poets take the allegorical sense (for St. Thomas the typological) in a way different from that of the theologians. In his rendering, the allegorical and moral senses are not very different from each other. The literal, which in a fictive work cannot refer to history in the same way as the Bible was said to, is "that sense which does not go beyond the strict limits of the letter" and the "sense which we get through the letter" (Aligheri, 1318/1971: 121, 122). These definitions apparently did not seem problematic to Dante: the literal conveys what happened, about which there need be no difficulty. Thus, with respect to his own *Commedia*, he writes, "The subject of the whole work, then, taken in the literal sense only is 'the state of souls after death,' without qualification, for the whole progress of the work hinges on it and about it" (p. 122).

Modern criticism begins to make the literal problematic, and that marks the completion of a shift away from a criticism concerned mainly with subject matter and only secondarily with technique or what Dante called "the form of the treatment" as against "the form of the treatise" (p. 122). This division and the resultant emphasis on content or subject matter follow out of theories of rhetoric on the one hand and emphasis on allegory on the other. Both instructed readers over centuries in what to look for and ways to order texts. It may not be true that, as D. W. Robertson (1963) tried to show, medieval literature, including Chaucer, was ordered on principles like Dante's, but clearly a theory of polysemy led readers to look for levels of significance. In the same way, the formal ordering of tropes back at least to Quintilian and the attitude that they were only devices of persuasion and delight emphasized an abstractable content.

There are cases where critics and readers (and the audiences of drama) seemed to give equal importance to formal matters, as in the French neoclassical drama with its rigid unities of time and space or the various forms of the Renaissance sonnet. At this point, the fourfold principle of polysemy was forgotten, and readers learned other paradigms. Clearly the neoclassical standards of Corneille and others gave an informed class of play-goers a definite idea of what to expect or at least a limiting range of expectations, and to some extent played the role in the area of form that the fourfold system had in the area of content.

I have noticed that difficulty or obscurity (at least of a certain allegorical kind) was regarded by some as a positive virtue. The negative concept of difficulty arises when it is thought that the author has overstepped the bounds of decorum. The earliest secular complaint about literary obscurity that I know is that of John Dryden about the poems of John Donne, who, he claimed, "perplexes the minds of the fair sex with nice speculations of philosophy when he should engage their hearts, and entertain them with the softness of love" (Dryden, 1693/1962: 76). Dryden accuses Donne of a breach of decorum with respect to the love lyric. He condescendingly attributes a confusion, which is perhaps his own, to women readers. The charge is that Donne breached the rules of genre by means of an inappropriate complexity of thought. His remark indicates that the "metaphysical" style had introduced new problems for readers. It is not exactly that poets before them had not been philosophical. They had, but the proper way had been to be allegorical. Indeed, the poet had always been different from the philosopher, as Sir Philip Sidney (1595/1971) remarked, partly because his work was more readily understandable:

> I say the philosopher teacheth, but he teacheth obscurely, so as the learned only can understand him; that is to say, he teacheth them that are already taught. But the poet is the food for the tenderest stomachs, the poet is indeed the right proper philosopher. [p. 161]

Sidney goes on to elicit the "pretty allegories" of Aesop's fables as proper examples (p. 161). For him, obscurity seems not a problem. For Dryden reading Donne it is, and there was not a lot more adjustment to Donne a century later when Samuel Johnson described the "metaphysical" style:

> The most heterogeneous ideas are yoked by violence together; nature and art are ransacked for illustrations, comparisons, and allusions; their learning instructs, and their subtlety surprises; but the reader commonly thinks his improvement dearly bought, and, though he sometimes admires, is seldom pleased. [Johnson, 1783/1964: 2–3]

Not very much was obscure to Dr. Johnson, but his remark certainly suggests that these poets' outlandishness was a difficulty for the reader. The revival of Donne in the early twentieth century was accomplished, amid bitter charges of obscurity, by T. S. Eliot and the New Criticism, which introduced a concept of irony that went far toward teaching readers what was going on in Donne's verse and to appreciate the very violence that Johnson was skeptical about and Dryden offended by.

Donne's poetry became identified with the experimental mood of modernist poetry dominated for a while by Eliot, and virtually every New Critic tried his hand at a reading of "The Canonization," making familiar to a generation of students the eccentricities of a style long out of fashion. It is convenient and perhaps right enough to think of all literature as composed of conventional and experimental elements (sometimes the conventional elements are the ground of experiment) or, as Eliot (1932) called these elements, "tradition" and "individual talent" (p. 3–11). Certainly since the romantic movement, and probably since Dryden wrote of Donne, and before, experiment has worked powerfully to make obscurity and difficulty important issues in criticism and practical issues in pedagogy.

"Experiment" is a word first associated with science, and it is not surprising that as a concept in art it followed on the burst of scientific activity in the Renaissance. It is also not surprising that obscurity as a critical issue of considerable magnitude follows experiment. Experiment comes with the unsettling of allegorical practices and tastes codified in the Middle Ages and tending to separate content from form with content privileged. The pact between author and reader begins to unravel at the same time that the number of readers, authors, and books increases dramatically. There begins, with Alexander Baumgarten's (1750) invention of the idea of "aesthetic," a new insistence on special values for literary art. It tends to turn the relation of content to form to one privileging form or insisting on the indissoluability of the relation between the two in any account of meaning. The movements challenged both authors and readers to establish new paradigms. Authors and readers cannot do without recognizable conventions. Shifts in conventions can be very disturbing and lead to charges of obscurity and the experience of difficulty—until the shifts become recognized and new behavior described or recognized as a revival of some kind.

I have concentrated on the early allegorists and typologists because their methods, developed and employed over centuries and put to work on the most revered texts, helped establish paradigms for reading of a certain sort and exemplify the work of paradigms in readerly practice. These paradigms were gradually abandoned, creating the need for new ones and for their recovery in order to read early literature with intelligence. The rise of experiment and individualism as literary values required in certain ways a new set of readerly expectations. But at the same time, literary conventions apparently overthrown have a way of persisting. In *Anatomy of Criticism,* Northrop Frye (1957) amusingly writes of Walt Whitman's remark about his elegy on Lincoln:

> He was right, being the kind of poet he was, in making the content of his own *When Lilacs Last in the Dooryard Bloomed* an elegy on Lincoln and not a conventional Adonis lament. Yet his elegy is, in its form, as conventional as *Lycidas,* complete with purple flowers thrown on coffins, a great star drooping in the west, imagery of "ever returning spring" and all the rest. [1957: 102]

Readers could read without difficulty what has become one of our most memorable poems because of its elegiac qualities, which they recognized.

II.

The first poet I know of to challenge openly a set of prevailing conventions was William Wordsworth in his 1800 preface to the second edition of *Lyrical Ballads*. Before Wordsworth, poets tended to identify themselves with a prevailing tradition and set of practices even though their own might have been somewhat eccentric. We today are so used to the concept of experiment that by now the term "convention" has a pejorative ring. Wordsworth rightly thought that he had to explain "poems so materially different from those upon which general approbation is at present bestowed" (Wordsworth, 1800/1971: 434). Years later he wrote, somewhat wistfully perhaps, of the need of a poet to create the taste by which he is eventually appreciated. Wordsworth overthrew received assumptions about poetic diction and consciously adopted, with important and sly variations, conventions of popular ballads. This move was made possible by the interest in ballads that was exemplified by Thomas Percy's *Reliques of Ancient English Poetry* (1765).

Criticism in the form of testaments by poets to their own methods has frequently been responsible for the initial training of readers to read works that disrupt the dominant sense of what literature properly is or does. This criticism divides mostly into two kinds. First, there is criticism of the "make it new" variety, which takes a militant stand against outworn convention. A large part of Wordsworth's preface is of this sort, particularly those passages that inveigh against standard poetic diction and defend his own practices. Such manifestos tend to identify reform with return to some version of common language and some version of the natural. One discovers similar strategies in Whitman, Pound, Kerouac, and Olson. This is not to say that these poets abandon all convention, only that they do not emphasize it. Often they adopt with a difference conventions not practiced by their immediate predecessors or conventions not regarded among those predecessors as quite proper, as in the case of Wordsworth with the ballad. (Sir Philip Syndey, in "An Apology for Poetry," 1595/1971, confesses to his own "barbarousness" when he writes of being moved by the ballad of "Chevy Chase"; 166.) Sometimes they invert the dominant convention, as George Bernard Shaw did when in his plays he made the hero take the heroine role, the wise man, the fool, and the like. American literature since Thoreau has had a strong tradition of unconventionality generated by a desire to free itself from Europe, creating its own conventions. This leads us to a second kind of criticism, which advocates a literature that is traditional while at the same it seems strange, daring, and revolutionary. Often technical invention is compensated for by symbolic traditionalism or vice versa. Thus William Blake, who wrote short poems meant to be sung like popular ballads and longer works with eccentric prosodic elements, depended heavily on the Bible and Milton for his symbolic materials. His methods seem to have taken something from the syncretic mythographers of his and a preceding generation, aligning him with tradition.

One of the major experimentalists of modernism, T. S. Eliot, astonished the literary world with *The Waste Land* and its mixed versification, its parodies, its allusiveness, and its footnotes. In his criticism he emphasized the importance of tradition even to the point of insisting that when a poet seems most individualistic, he is then likely to be most traditional. Eliot played a major role in the revival of Donne, the modernist criticism of Renaissance drama, and the molding of a taste that would make the acceptance of great modernists like James Joyce possible. His is a didactic criticism emphasizing historical continuity. In his own work he seems deliberately to have put his experimentalism to the business of restoring interest (with a difference) in the literature of certain past ages. His footnotes to *The Waste Land*, themselves an eccentricity, seem to imply that readers should recognize his allusions to past works, but that, alas, they are not likely to; the footnotes are, therefore, a sign of traditionalism after all. It is a mistake to think of them as appendages to or comments on the poem. They are part of it and pursue the same ends as the rest of the poem.

Eliot is one of the last influential nonacademic poet-critics. No one today outside the academy holds a like position. This may be evidence of a "natural" evolution. Eliot was certainly a didactic critic seeking to teach people how to read in his time, addressing problems he thought central to reading in that time. Education having become almost entirely institutional, it is not surprising that didactic criticism is now written mostly by academics. Furthermore, a combination of academic specialization and "creative" writers' identification of themselves as in antithetical opposition to the culture at large or to the strongest forces in it has tended to split writers from the practice of criticism, which has in a variety of ways become more rigid in its own conventions since its entrance into academia. The critic-teacher, unlike Hazlitt, Lamb, or Coleridge, is now in the classroom, and problems of reading are being addressed even by people who, as Auden wryly commented in a poem, "commit a social science."

This has happened in a time when the concept of literary originality, invented during the romantic movement, has itself become a convention and even a cliché of writers. It has happened in a time when the educational process has tended to ignore, often deliberately, those matters that, if taken up in a serious way, would contribute to a capacity to read literary works with greater ease. Latin and Greek have virtually disappeared from the curriculum and with them a principal vehicle for the teaching of English etymology. History has succumbed to social science and an emphasis on the present. With these things the likelihood of spotting allusions and grasping the richness of most words and many aspects of works of the past has diminished. Few students learn any terms with which to formulate a sense of literary verse forms, and memorization is no longer a pedagogical technique, so that people rarely have a store of rhythms in mind.

On the other hand, the introduction of modernist literature into the curriculum and the serious teaching of criticism and theory have made students more likely to accept experimental works. (It is not often understood that the developments in criticism and theory of the past sixty or seventy years have been principally pedagogic in intent and a reaction to habits of scholarship fairly remote from effective interpretive teaching.) One might add that since students today often have less knowledge and experience of literary conventions and traditions, they come to the literature they read with fewer conventional expectations. All of this may seem to lead in the direction of openness of response, and may in some degree actually so lead. But it also generates or allows to exist a radical temporal provincialism like that of some isolated tribe. This helps to vitiate the gains of openness.

More recently developments in literature and theoretical speculation about literature and language have threatened to unsettle pedagogical practices that have only recently adjusted to some of the major effects of modernism. One senses a situation in which a few students are ahead of their teachers and institutions insofar as they have a sort of intuitive grasp of postmodernist literary practice without any language to express it. The reason for this is that such practices are reflected in popular art, television, and advertising, with which the young are saturated. But most students have been so cut loose from literary tradition that they are completely at sea when faced with a text.

No literature or criticism can exist without the literary past. Experiment always experiments against something and thus depends on it for its antithetical quality. Wolfgang Iser begins a recent book on Laurence Sterne's *Tristram Shandy,* one of the great radical experiments in English literature, with a chapter "Does *Tristram Shandy* have a beginning?," which is a question you cannot ask if you did not know that there have been beginnings in a certain sense. Iser (1988) mentions *Tristram Shandy* as "a landmark of narrative literature despite its flagrant breach of convention." So *Tristram Shandy* counts on, brings into itself, so to speak, all the texts that do have conventional beginnings. The same with endings and with the concept of closure. You cannot give significance to openness if there is no notion of closure to be different from.

Readers read well, then, because they have read already—that is, have learned the conventions that the text of the moment follows, undermines, parodies, rejects, or ignores. Conventions are always present, even in their absence. Conventions are, of course, of various sorts and are differently emphasized in various works and traditions. Within the larger emphases of content and form or subject matter and technique are the categories of symbolic conventions, which in recent times have been the province of a criticism that emphasizes myth and archetype (or repeated convention). The great theorist of this kind of criticism has been Northrop Frye, and Frye has always been eager to claim that his work is most relevant to what ought to be the concerns of the teachers of the youngest children, since it begins with the symbolic patterns of myth, legend, and folktale that form the basis of children's stories and are endlessly repeated in popular literature and drama.

Formal verse patterns have been the subject of study for centuries in English back to the work of George Puttenham (in his *The Arte of English Poesie*, 1968/1589) and his contemporaries. In recent times, with developments in free verse, there may have been a tendency to underplay the importance of understanding traditional forms. But, as seems to be inevitable, free verse began to look like a convention itself, and there has now developed a literature about it (see especially Hartman, 1980), emphasizing its techniques and connecting it by contrast and parallel to what had preceded it, which includes Blake's and Hopkins's experiments. Most students do not have very much patience with discussions of prosody and the like, or at least they have trouble with descriptive systems of some complexity. Those that do not are more likely to have read poetry or to have been read to at an early age so that certain rhythmic conventions are part of their memory in actual verse forms.

Spatio-temporal conventions, of great interest in what is now called narrative theory, are much more complicated than criticism for a long time noticed. When it got around to discussing prose fiction, the New Criticism, following the lead of Henry James's conscious practice and Percy Lubbock's commentary on him and others (James, 1948; Lubbock, 1921), emphasized the matter of focus of narration and point of view, while nearly concurrently the deployment of time became almost an obsession with certain modernist writers. The behavior of narrators became of utmost importance, and narrative acts began to be dwelt upon in critical texts as much as what was narrated. Much good teaching is simply the pointing out and harping on something that is obvious once attention is drawn to it. That is the case with narrative behavior. Readers have now learned to ask questions early on about narrators: Who is speaking? Or is he or she writing? Where? When? Who is listening? Reading? Such questions imply critical conventions and a narrative paradigm.

Then, of course, some writer comes along who makes a work that does not seem to have a narrator at all, but just "narration," so that the paradigmatic questions are not adequate. In such cases two things worth mentioning here are involved: first, such writings would be far less meaningful if the old questions had not been asked and we did not know they had been asked; second, such works often send us back to certain earlier ones, which in this new light reveal an interesting aspect previously ignored. These are reasons why the history of critical practice should be studied concurrently with the history of literature. Many people think the history of criticism and theory has little to do with real literary study or with the teaching of how to read a text well. It has everything to do with it, especially when one presumes that error is instructive.

Spatio-temporal conventions in literature are often closely related to what is going on at any given time in the other arts and in the sciences. Until the romantic period the emphasis was spatial and the principal analogue of literature was painting. Horace's so-called speaking picture was a cliché of criticism. This fitted well with Newtonian science. Romanticism invented the analogy with music. "All art aspires to the condition of music" is a phrase attributed to more than one nineteenth-century writer. Both the Horatian dictum and this are profoundly suggestive pedagogical statements even today, though they were more or less polemical when they were uttered. That is, like any good analogy, they reveal a lot about possible ways of reading. Successful readers respond to or develop such analogies, which both expand and limit interpretation.

The preromantic emphasis was not just vaguely spatial; it was spatial in a Newtonian and Euclidian sense, and where the emphasis on temporality came in time was itself at first strongly spatialized. Even the memory was seen in the forms of Lockean and Hartleyan associationist psychology, spatial in ways that had not yet heard of the paradoxicality of space in the later physics. The next stage of temporality came with new developments in biology and with analogies between literature and musical structures.

Such analogies border on what we conventionally call allusions. Students not much experienced in past literature are sometimes aware of allusiveness but often not of the allusion and its referent. Student readers of Shakespeare, Milton, Pope, and Wordsworth often think at first that these poets are uttering clichés, not knowing that they originated certain later well-used phrases. Sometimes they attribute a phrase to some later allusion outside literature as did the student who marveled to me when she discovered the phrase "splendor in the grass" in Wordsworth. She had first seen it as a movie title.

Literary allusiveness is, of course, by no means always literary and ranges broadly into all facts of life. Readers' capacities here are related not just to how much literature they have read but to how much they have learned about the world. Students who often seem totally insensitive to allusions in writing are extremely alert to spoken allusion and nuance. It is to a great extent a matter of experience.

Yet an immense knowledge of conventions and traditions, history, science, and the fine arts will not alone guarantee the reader's capacity to deal with tomorrow's writing or even that of just previous generations; for writers are making it new even as they use the past. Such texts may be obscure because our paradigms do not quite contain them. Luckily there are academic critics paid to struggle with such texts, to try to build adequate paradigms that can help readers learn how to read a new range of works. Among critics, themselves, there is the same problem of the inadequate paradigm. Indeed, no paradigm is adequate in the sense that it can totally unlock meaning even for now, let alone for all time. Nevertheless, what we call obscurity is often simply that for which at the time we do not have an adequate paradigm.

As I have already suggested, contemporary students are often open to dealing with this situation even as they seem less formally equipped than their predecessors to do so. That Joyce's *Ulysses* is now an extremely popular subject for a course, and that his *Finnegans Wake* becomes so where it is taught, seem to indicate this. In the case of *Finnegans Wake*, however, there may be another reason: the very same modernist devices used in *Finnegans Wake* and certain other works of the time have influenced popular entertainment—the movies, television, and perhaps, most sophisticated of all, advertising. Thus students have gained some acquaintance with modernist conventions somewhat watered down at second hand. Indeed, so-called postmodernism is to a large extent characterized by the massive use of devices present in *Finnegans Wake* and rock videos.

When *Ulysses* and *Finnegans Wake* first appeared, they confounded many critics. Joyce himself, fearing misunderstanding, leaked the key to the Homeric theme to Stuart Gilbert after he had talked about it during composition with Frank Budgen (Budgen, 1934; Gilbert, 1930). The first phase of *Ulysses* criticism involved trying to get all that straight and to follow out the implications of what seemed to be a sort of untraditional table of correspondences. The risk was always that the text would be overschematized, making Joyce into a kind of diagrammatist, the very thing that he most decidedly was not. Eventually Gilbert's tables of correspondences seemed to be exhausted as means to understand the text and became counterproductive.

The next significant phase was that of minute attention to conventions of narrative, and this proved fruitful. (This phase includes work by Wolfgang Iser, Dorrit Cohn, Jean Paul Riquelmé, and Karen Lawrence. For my own essay on this subject, see Adams, 1985–86.) But rather than starting out in this way with *Finnegans Wake*, criticism like George Eliot's Casaubon again tried to find the key to Joycean mythology. The first books again sought a system (see Cambell and Robinson, 1944; Hart, 1962). They were not very successful, except that they were written by very intelligent people who had occasional insights about parts of the text in spite of a questionable paradigm.

Later on it began to be seen that *Finnegans Wake* was not the system that Joyce made in order to escape someone else's. It was the antithesis of system as we usually think of system, and Joyce was having great fun leading its readers down false conceptual trails. This was an authorial mind determined to frustrate critical system-making. It had gone beyond the narrative strategies of *Ulysses,* where the concept of a narrator had been expanded to include several narrators and then an overseeing "arranger," who became a sort of character in the text. In *Finnegans Wake* this arranger became a "deranger," one might say, or simply narration deranged. It seemed possible at the same time to claim that Joyce was working not on the edges of literature but was expanding its very center insofar as the center of literature may be marked by resistance to system-atization, which becomes identified with the assumption that language as a system built on logical and empirical principles provides a stable impression of a world already out there.

But what if language, and especially literary language, operates not so much as a representer of a world out there as a form in which we try to constitute our experience of a world that may or may not be graspable in any simple way? What if, further, language bears within itself some sort of resistance to simple representation? That would make language much more difficult right on the face of it! We would have to ask much more probing questions about what language is doing if it is not copying some presumed prelinguistic world. Our assumptions about what an interpretation is would have to change, and we might see literature not as a copier of nature but a constitutor of our culture. It would be the place we could learn what we have made and are making of the world of human activity. It would be there to tell us what we are as a society; and, because much literature is self-consciously fictive and even fantastic, it would be there to tell us what we hope for and fear. We would be looking for something different, acting on different premises when we read, and such shifts of premises are difficult.

In this case it would mean that we must abandon the assumption that we need to read through a text to the reality on the other side that is being copied, whether that reality is declared to be nature, moral, or physical truth, or even God and the sacred. We would be trying to get clear in our minds a version of verbal culture, not ultimate truths that recede infinitely down every chain of metaphor that we pursue. The difficulty of reading this way is the difficulty of overcoming certain traditional and apparently quite natural assumptions that do not hold up to scrutiny once one begins to query language itself.

In earlier ages, criticism, and nearly everyone, assumed as unproblematic the copy theory of language, and if a literary work seemed to violate this assumption, it was quickly regarded as an allegory in which system and truth were hidden by a variety of cunning devices. Many literary works, like *The Faerie Queene*, had just enough allegory or the apparent susceptibility to allegorical reading that critics could construct meaning in this way. But beginning with romanticism both literature and criticism are strewn with practices and manifestos resisting allegory or critical allegorizing (though often falling into it in practice). This resistance becomes the central defining feature of literature for at least one type of romantic and postromantic sensibility. *Finnegans Wake* is powerfully resistant to allegorization, yet it is a text that knows it must, to gain its ends, presume a tradition of allegorical reading. It even contains a parody of such reading. Over and over it seems to be setting out toward expression of a mappable system. Over and over at the crucial moment, within sentence, within paragraph, within chapter, within book, it wanders from the route that for a while readers presume it to have taken.

Even Samuel Beckett, one of Joyce's heirs, whose early essay on *Finnegans Wake* remains valuable, tried to find a system of sorts by recourse to the thought of Giordano Bruno. But to express this relationship shows in the end that only the antithetical aspects of Bruno are retained in *Finnegans Wake*.

What are the implications for a reasonably common feeling among postmodernist readers who have attempted to read it that *Finnegans Wake* approaches a sort of center of literature? Before I try to answer that, I have to notice that postmodernism, at least in its deconstructionist forms, tends to reject the idea of "literature" as a special body of texts and the idea of a "center" as the very notion of truth that I have just called in question as available to language. One can, however, use the term "center" to mean a metaphorical place where there is exhibited most completely and intensively those characteristics of language that actually work against the simple notion of copying and representation. This is to say that *Finnegans Wake* challenges us to confront the possibilities of language in a new way. It is a test of the way we have learned to read, which, I have implied, is mainly the learning of literary conventions.

Finnegans Wake makes us rethink what a critical paradigm needs to be. As such, it appears as a puzzle, but without a solution in the usual sense. Rather we learn from it through its very resistance to what we may have thought learning was. We are not the same in our relation to language and therefore to culture. All this is difficult, but no intelligent critic ever wholly denied that literature has its insidious and subversive side. As we rethink, we enlarge our idea of language itself, and one result is that we begin to read other and earlier works in more expansive ways. We also occasionally discover works neglected or misunderstood in ages tied to copy theories.

III.

Reading, then, is properly characterized by movement. There is no key to unlock a space of learnable rules or methods that we could long inhabit. If what I have been saying has any truth to it, learning to read literary texts is hampered by a tacit pedagogical presumption that we must begin with so-called easy texts and gradually work toward more obviously complex ones. This is the parallel in pedagogy to the idea that scholarship should establish once and for all the text and the historical and biographical context before writers should hazard an interpretation. If this principle is rigorously held to, criticism never begins, for texts are rarely finally established and contexts are infinite in possibility. Some generations of scholars avoided interpretive talk except in the most general way. I recall one of my undergraduate classes in which the professor, lecturing on Marvell's "To His Coy Mistress," told us about Marvell's life, certain stylistic characteristics that linked him to the "metaphysical" poets, and some of the politics of the age. Then in the waning moments of the hour, he read the poem aloud, remarking reverently that it was very good. I quarrel only with the limits of such an approach and the assumptions behind the created limits.

Today we do not have the tendency infinitely to defer interpretation. The New Criticism pretty well put an end to that. But in the wake of its great inventive critics came a horde of academic scholars practicing a method of interpretation that quickly surpassed in sheer bulk the whole body of biblical readings, domesticating into a dull academic exercise a movement that began in the excitement of new ideas imaginatively pursued.

At about the same time, complex developments in society and education resulted in our tendency to defer students' reading of so-called difficult texts, with the result that for some time now those in college often have not proceeded very far to grasp literary conventions, which is to say that they have great trouble reading almost any text, "literature" or not. This is not helped by the disappearance of the classics and by the great reluctance any teacher is likely to have to deal with the Bible anywhere in the curriculum.

The problem begins, I suspect, with the choice of the earliest texts in the primary grades, goes on with the search for "readable" and doctrinally neutral texts, and extends into college courses in so-called popular literature and children's literature. Teachers of these courses have found that the best and perhaps only way to teach courses on these subjects is to discuss their use of conventions of plot, character types, and imagery, principally because such texts are very conventional. Thus in some ways teachers find themselves in those courses to be compensating for an early lack.

If language is as complicated as linguists, philosophers, and critics like to tell us, then it almost appears that what we call literary education is deliberately trying, like the old priesthoods, to hide something from students.

One of the things that clearly needs to be treated with particular respect to recent literature, but really to all, is the role that tropes play in language. This is a subject I do not have the space to discuss here, but clearly there is a history of the way tropes have been regarded over time that is as important as the way allegory has been regarded. Indeed, allegory itself is a trope in that history, though the history of metaphor is closer to what I am concerned with. One discovers here a history of tropical conventions (see Ricoeur, 1977). The history of metaphor is central to the history of language. As far as I know, the history of language, including how language changes and the constitutive role it plays in culture, is a subject never mentioned in secondary education and not much discussed with undergraduate college students.

The historical and social study of language is a difficult, knotty, puzzling subject. It is also of extraordinary importance, since we all live in language and speak it; and it, as philosophers have observed, speaks us. What could be more important to gain some understanding of? Even to gain some understanding of the puzzling nature of language—to recognize its mysteriousness—is important. I have spent what some readers may regard as an inordinate amount of time on the history of interpretation in this paper. The history of interpretation is an important part of the history of language itself, and we come to understand the situation of reading and of difficulty by grasping the story of human grappling with that situation.

In these last few paragraphs the implication is that the difficulty of difficulty is not that it is difficult but that we do not face difficulty soon enough. Two problems arise as a result. First, we lose the opportunity to take advantage of the fascination of difficulty itself. If we go into a toy store, we discover shelves of puzzles of considerable complexity. Children love them. What about puzzles do they love? It has to be the difficulty and the process of overcoming it. (I shall say more about this shortly.) Second, to put off difficulty as puzzle is to increase difficulty in the same way that we increase immeasurably the difficulty of learning a foreign language when we delay it past the earliest grades in school.

There is a third problem that I shall relate specifically to reading. We too often take some variation of the position Dryden took against Donne, which is to prolong not just ignorance but to applaud superficiality in the name of decorum. The result of this situation for college teachers of literature is a paradoxical one.

Suppose one tried to study a few pages of *Finnegans Wake* with some college freshmen. What would the situation be? All the students would probably be confounded and declare themselves helpless, but they would divide into three different groups. The first would think, though unable to express the matter clearly, that this was not literature, because there was no hold to get on it by application of whatever conventions they knew. The second would not be sophisticated enough to think in these terms, but some of them (and here is the paradox), because of their innocence to some extent, would be intrigued and unencumbered by the presumptions of the first group. They would have to be told what it means to overturn conventions and how that works in the text. This would involve discussion of the conventions themselves. Presumably, in the best of pedagogical worlds, the two groups would come together after a while. The third group would be perhaps the most interesting and challenging, though maybe not the most difficult to teach. This would be the group that had by a sort of osmosis picked up quite a few conventions from our most popular and ubiquitous arts: advertising and television, including rock video. These things tend to be very conventional and very contemporary, which means that they lag behind the contemporary avant-garde of literature and water down literary complexity for purposes of immediate and vulgar, which is to say in this country commercial, effect.

Anyone brought up on "I Love Lucy" and "Mr. Ed" is bound to be puzzled and disoriented by rock videos in a way not unfamiliar to people brought up on Hardy and Hemingway who have opened *Finnegans Wake*. I have used *Finnegans Wake* in college classes and discovered that modest gains can be made with it in teaching how to read a literary text. This, it turns out, is to offer students a puzzle and engage them in the dialectic of convention and variation or revolt. Extreme texts, not at the periphery but in the center, and therefore strange, are actually quite useful for this endeavor. Of course, one has to be able to recognize the difficulty as a puzzle—a puzzle, in the case of literature, without an allegorical key or the expected kind of solution. Students need to come to understand that to read a text is never a terminal event like the placement of the last jigsaw piece. To learn this and be able to live with it and be satisfied with it is itself a solution.

Coleridge observed quite correctly that with literature the process of reading, which he characterized as a journey, is properly more important than the destination. Many years ago the New Critics attacked the "heresy of paraphrase," claiming that poems do not have paraphrastic solutions. The recent movement known as deconstruction says this again with greater insistence and application to all kinds of texts. This movement notices something about the particular difficulty, or mysteriousness, of language itself, not just poetry. It is a mystery that can turn into a fascination in the classroom, if students can be made to realize how much of our life is involved in language. Under such conditions *Finnegans Wake* and many relatively recent texts that are about language even as they are about life can be made to yield up a fascinating difficulty.

In any learning to read, one needs to come fairly soon to the realization that one's subjectivity is alone not of much critical value and that literature in general does not operate according to the subject-object paradigm, which was invented and sustained by a strongly antiliterary scientific outlook. The aim of the reader of literature should be attainment of a position, never in fact reachable. I have elsewhere called it the position of the "authoritively projected reader" (Adams, 1983: 242–64). Every text demands (and this may be a demand that the author has not explicitly made) an effort of reading that takes readers outside themselves to a position transcending the old personal limits and foibles of taste. Readers are challenged to be the readers that the text demands. A grasp of conventions is a help in this. That is, however, only the beginning, and there is no ending.

Blake in his difficult so-called prophetic books suggests a phrase for what he regarded as the greatest of ethical acts: annihilation of the selfhood. To try to become the reader that the text demands is a movement toward such annihilation, which is ethical because it is an effort to break out of one's subjectivity into an area where one can identify oneself with others who have tried to do the same. In the most intense of such experiences, a moment in a class on *Finnegans Wake*, in an audience at *King Lear*, at those times when we sense something has truly happened, and it is possible to express to each other something of it in nearly adequate words, we achieve a sort of ethical bond, which is the best reason for the critical effort that I know.

REFERENCES

Adams, H. (1983). *Joyce Cary's trilogies*. Tallahassee: Florida State University Press.

Adams, H. (1985–6). "Critical constitution of the literary text." *New Literary History*, 17, 595–616.

Alighieri, D. (1304–8/1971). "The banquet." In H. Adams, ed., *Critical theory since Plato*. New York: Harcourt Brace Jovanovich.

———. (1318/1971). "Letter to can grande della scala." In H. Adams, ed., *Critical theory since Plato*. New York: Harcourt Brace Jovanovich.

Aquinas, T. (1256–72/1971). "The nature and domain of sacred doctrine." In H. Adams, ed., *Critical theory since Plato*. New York: Harcourt Brace Jovanovich.

Auerbach, E. (1959). *Scenes from the drama of European literature.* New York: Meridian Books.

Baumgarten, A. (1750/1936). *Aesthetica.* Bari, Italy: J. Laterza and Sons.

Bigg, C. (1968). *The Christian Platonists of Alexandria.* Oxford: Clarendon Press.

Budgen, F. (1934). *James Joyce and the making of Ulysses.* Bloomington: Indiana University Press.

Campbell, J., and Robinson, H. M. (1944). *A skeleton key to Finnegans Wake.* New York: Harcourt, Brace.

Chadwick, H. (1966). *Early Christian thought and the classical tradition: Studies in Justin, Clement, and Origen.* New York: Oxford University Press.

Daniélou, J. (1960). *From shadows to reality: Studies in the biblical typology of the fathers.* Westminster, Md.: Newman Press.

Dryden, J. (1693/1962). "A discourse concerning the original and progress of satire." In G. Watson, ed., *Of dramatic poesy and other critical essays* (vol. 2). London: Everyman's Library.

Eliot, T.S. (1932). *Selected essays, 1917–1932.* New York: Harcourt Brace.

Fairbairn, (1852/1956). *The typology of scripture.* Grand Rapids: Zondervan.

Frye, N. (1957). *Anatomy of criticism.* Princeton: Princeton University Press.

———. (1963). *Fables of identity.* New York: Harcourt Brace and World.

Gilbert, S. (1930). *James Joyce's Ulysses.* New York: Albert A. Knopf.

Glatzer, N. M., ed. (1971). *The essential Philo.* New York: Schocken Books.

Goodenough, E. R. (1962). *Introduction to Philo Judaeus.* New York: Barnes and Noble.

Hart, C. (1962). *Structure and motif in Finnegans Wake.* London: Faber and Faber.

Hartman, C. O. (1980). *Free verse: An essay in prosody.* Princeton: Princeton University Press.

Iser, W. (1988). *Laurence Stern: Tristram Shandy* (D. H. Wilson, Trans.). Cambridge: Cambridge University Press.

James, H. (1948). *The art of the novel.* New York: Charles Scribner's Sons.

Johnson, S. (1783/1964). "The life of Abraham Cowley." In W. Fleis-chauer, ed., *Lives of the English poets, selections.* Chicago: Henry Regnery.

Lubbock, (1921). *The craft of fiction.* London: Jonathan Cape.

Puttenham, G. (1589/1968). *The arte of English poesie.* R.C. Alston,, ed. Menston, England: Scolar Press Limited.

Raine, K. (1968). *Blake and tradition* (vols. 1–2). Princeton: Princeton University Press.

Raine, K., and Harper, G., eds. (1969). *Thomas Taylor the Platonist.* Princeton: Princeton University Press.

Reynolds, H. (1632/1971). "Mythomystes." In H. Adams, ed., *Critical theory since Plato.* New York: Harcourt Brace Jovanovich.

Ricoeur, (1977). *The rule of metaphor.* Toronto: University of Toronto Press.

Robertson, D. W., Jr. (1963). *A preface to Chaucer.* London: Oxford University Press.

Sidney, (1595/1971). "An apology for poetry." In H. Adams, ed., *Critical theory since Plato.* New York: Harcourt Brace Jovanovich.

Sowers, S. G. (1965). *The hermeneutics of Philo and Hebrews.* Zurich: EVX.

Wordsworth, W. (1800/1971). Preface to the second edition of *Lyrical ballads.* In H. Adams, ed., *Critical theory since Plato.* New York: Harcourt Brace Jovanovich.

3.

Literary Theory and the Notion of Difficulty

William Touponce

THE THEORY OF THE TEXT

My charge in this paper is to review the implications of current literary theory and theoretical views of the text for determining the nature of text difficulty and reading proficiency. This in itself is a topic of some difficulty. Modern literary theory is a large and often arcane area; no one, I think, could claim competence in all its diverse idioms, or even an easy familiarity with them. Indeed, as often as not, theorists today are apt to write on the sublime difficulties of mastering just one critical idiom in all its current ramifications. (See Hertz, 1985. All of the essays in this series reflect the difficulty of mastering textuality with a metalanguage.) Nor can the "key words" approach do us much good in this situation, for as I. A. Richards observed, a certain familiarity with critical key words may breed contempt for the literary text and thereby block us from truly understanding it. And as a matter of fact, the theory of the text is for this very reason critical of any metalanguage—of any institutional mediator of meaning—a factor that makes it all the more difficult to present in a summary fashion. Nonetheless, I will attempt to discuss within a reasonably short space three theorists whose idioms have a certain currency in the Anglo-American academic community, or at least that part of it that concerns itself with theorizing on the process of reading literary texts.

I mean specifically the writings of French literary theorists and thinkers such as Jacques Lacan, Jacques Derrida, and Roland Barthes, who share a view that the text is the primary object of investigation and point of departure for any discipline in the human sciences, whether it be psychoanalysis (Lacan), philosophy (Derrida), or literary criticism and theory (Barthes). Where there is no text, there is no object of study, and no object of thought either. All three thinkers would agree with this statement, though they may present different views about the nature of textuality, and the difficulty of apprehending it, as they see it from their disciplines. I will discuss the problem of the text as each thinker defines it in the appropriate section below, but "text," at this early point of our investigation, is to be understood in the broadest sense as any coherent complex of signs.

How textuality has been explored by these three thinkers is my main theoretical concern in this paper, but I might mention at the outset that each of these thinkers has been involved with pedagogical reforms within institutions in French culture: Derrida with the teaching of philosophy, Lacan with a training institute in psychoanalysis and a famous seminar, and Barthes with the teaching of literature. Each has had provocative and sometimes discouraging things to say about the difficulties of apprehending textuality in an institutional context (Barthes went so far as to say that the theory of the text has little institutional future). They have made pronouncements of this sort because the theory of the text tends to abolish the separation of genres and arts on which the traditional university has been founded. For the theory of the text no longer considers works as mere "messages" transmitted from one generation to the next, or even as "statements"—that is, finished products whose destiny would be sealed as soon as they were uttered—but as "perpetual productions," enunciations through which a semiotically conceived subject continues to struggle (see Kristeva, 1980).

The central theme of this semiotic subject involved with textuality as we find it in Barthes, Derrida, and Lacan is that self-knowledge comes not from introspection, from an inquiry into a putative "inner world" of autonomous consciousness and sense-constituting acts (key themes in Husserlian phenomenology and criticism of consciousness as practiced by George Poulet and others of the Geneva school), but from reflection upon the field of expressions in which one finds oneself, individually and socially. (For an account of the Geneva school, see Lawall, 1968.) This subject is no doubt that of the author, but it is also that of the reader, and the theory of the text also tends to abolish the institutional barriers set between the two. In other words, the theory of the text brings with it a new epistemological object: reading, an object virtually disdained by the whole of French classical criticism and the American New Criticism as well, which never had any but the most meager conception of the reader whose relation to the work was thought to be one of projection.

For French critics such as Roland Barthes, a literary text is one species of the social institution called *écriture* (writing); what makes it literary is the fact that the writing embodies a set of specifically literary conventions and codes. But while Barthes agrees that it is important to know these codes, the activity of *lecture* (reading), as he conceives it, should not allow itself to be entirely constrained by the literary conventions and codes that went into the writing. On the contrary, the theory of the text authorizes us to read works of the past with an entirely modern gaze and insists strongly on the productive equivalence of reading and writing. Furthermore, reading is not to be conceived of as a mere act of consumption. Full reading for Barthes would involve *plaisir/jouissance* in which the reader is nothing less than the one who desires to write, to give him/herself up to an erotic practice of language (see discussion of pleasure in reading below).

In other words the theory of the text suggests that the idea of difficulty is less a property of texts themselves than of the ways in which institutions train us to read:

> The theory of the text can find historical indications in the use of reading; it is certain that contemporary civilization tends to flatten reading out, by making it into a simple consumption, entirely separated from writing. Not only does the school system boast that it teaches reading, and no longer as in former times writing (even if the pupil or student of those days had to write according to a highly conventionalized rhetorical code), but also writing itself is driven off and confined in a caste of technicians (writers, teachers, intellectuals). [Barthes, 1981: 42]

Of course institutions (or communities, see Purves, in this volume) and the ways in which they train us to read is a subject of much critical debate in the United States recently. To give one example, I need only mention Robert Scholes's *Textual Power* (1985), which is an analysis of the entire English apparatus and how it could be reformed to overcome the split between composition and literature by using textual theory. Scholes is somewhat more hopeful than Barthes about the possibilities of institutional reform, but it is not my purpose here to assess these various projects or their feasibility (another is Gregory L. Ulmer's *Allied Grammatology*, 1985, using Derridean theory of the text). I will be discussing only the theory of the text as we find it in the works of Lacan, Derrida, and Barthes, and not the American appropriation of these works.

It is worth mentioning, however, that to the extent that Barthes was a reformist, he was inclined by personal temperament to a provisional, localized kind of reformism. For him, teaching would be directed toward "exploding" the literary text, tracing its codes and semantic fissures, examining the multiple ways in which any one literary text echoes, or is inescapably linked to, other texts, whether by open or covert citations and allusions, by the assimilation of features of an earlier text by a later text, or simply by participation in a common stock of literary codes and conventions. The teaching of literature would then be directed toward having students acquire a sensitivity to intertextuality, a term used by Julia Kristeva, but which ultimately stems from the writings of Mikhail

Bakhtin (see "The Problem of the Text" in Bakhtin, 1986.) I might add that to a thoroughgoing poststructuralist such as Barthes, the world itself can be "textualized":

> The pedagogical problem would be to shake up the literary notion of the text and to make adolescents understand that there is text everywhere, but that not everything is text; I mean that there is text everywhere, but that repetition, stereotype and *doxa* are also everywhere. That's the goal: the distinction between this textuality, which is not to be found only in literature, and society's neurotic, repetitive activity. [Barthes, 1985: 149]

Barthes's remarks that repetition, stereotype, and *doxa* (opinion, popular belief) are everywhere, and that students should be trained to see the difference between this and textuality per se, will be discussed later, but presently I want to point out that these remarks have an affinity of thought with those of I. A. Richards and his notion of the stock response—that is, fixed conventionalized reactions. Richards was the first Anglo-American literary critic to be largely concerned with the notion of difficulty in reading, and although his *Practical Criticism* (1929, though my references are to a 1963 edition) was written over a half-century ago, it still has relevance today. His peculiar mixture of Arnoldian high seriousness and positivism may seem old-fashioned, but that does not mean that we cannot learn from his methods—or from his hopes. Indeed, as we look back today with revisionary eyes at the intellectual figures who shaped cultural criticism in the twentieth century, Richards seems a prime target for rereading.

Something of this rereading is present in Geoffrey Hartman's *The Fate of Reading* (1975), in which Richards is a key intellectual figure leading to what Hartman calls our "dream of communication"—of total, controllable communication. Hartman points out that Richards was the first to diagnose how the modern heterogeneous growth of society—it includes the rise of other media—has "disordered" our ability to read. Richards's empirical studies of his students at Cambridge University, as they expressed themselves in protocols of reading, revealed the shocking and disturbing fact that many of them simply could not understand the "textuality" (Richards did not use this word, but I think that the notion is clearly operative in his comments) of poetry. They had difficulties on every level, from failure to make out the plain sense of a poem, to general critical preconceptions and prior demands made upon poetry as a result of theories, conscious or unconscious, about its nature and value.

Although Richards was disturbed by his findings, he did not believe that readers needed to be as helpless as his protocols showed them to be. On the contrary, the reader "ought to be given better defensive technique against the manifold bamboozlements of the world" (Richards, 1963: 74). The effect of *Practical Criticism* (which Richards called "fieldwork in comparative ideology") was to demonstrate that reading could not be taken as second nature any longer. In later books he tried to consider reading on a serious philosophical level. In these books Richards was the first critic to insist that in an age that, partly through social causes, was rapidly losing its ability to read with understanding, reflective inquiry into the reading of texts was necessary. He hoped that this reflective inquiry might lead to a theory by which the powers of reading might he regained "this time as a less vulnerable and more deeply grounded, because more consciously recognized, endowment" (Richards, 1935: 195).

But Hartman does not discuss the ways in which Richards's goals have themselves become institutionalized. That story is told in Elizabeth Freund's *The Return of the Reader* (1987), in which Richards also wins a place of respect and is seen as a constituting father figure who "is responsible, no matter how indirectly, for the way we read" (p. 38). In Freund's revisionary history, Richards begets the enemy brothers of reader-response criticism and "objective" formalist criticism at once. According to her, it was Richards's authentic respect for semantic instability and for the prodigality of verbal meaning, joined with his belief in the perfectibility of communication, that bred his aspiration to analyze, institutionalize, and thereby curb a seemingly uncontrollable proliferation of idiosyncratic readings, to "regulate" meaning (p. 43).

Freund goes on to show how Richards dealt with semantic plurality by proposing a four-part theory of meaning. We cannot grasp any utterance fully, Richards argues, unless we understand at least four different kinds of meaning (which he called sense, feeling, tone, and intention) and their interdependence upon one another. In ways similar to Barthes, the Richards of the *Practical Criticism* focuses our attention on the differences and ambiguities of the literary text (a project carried out by his student Empson). But of course he wants to regulate meaning in ways that Barthes, with his view of "exploding" the text, does not. Freund's retrospective account of Richards takes a much more skeptical view of him than Hartman does—"We do not solve problems by means of theory; only sort their components out differently" (p. 39)—but still admits that the *Practical Criticism* is a theoretical book of distinction.

In view of the importance of Richards to the Anglo-American tradition, I have used his categories of the difficulties involved in criticism—in a form modified and generalized by Purves and Beach in their *Literature and the Reader* (1972)—as a familiar point of reference throughout what follows. Purves and Beach found that the classification of problems in reading and understanding overlap a great deal and could be generalized into three schemata of understanding: information lack;

cognitive failure; and psychological block. In this paper I have dealt primarily with the second two schemata.

JACQUES LACAN AND THE TEXT OF FREUD

Freud's influence on his time does not necessarily reflect a close reading of his texts: his ideas were popularized, his jargon came into common usage (consider his influence on the modern literature of the fantastic, for example). But very often knowledge of his theories was secondhand, by way of critics or magazines. In lectures, essays, and seminars for over thirty years until the time of his death in 1981, Lacan had been urging a return to the letter of Freud's text. With Socratic irony ("I know that I don't know") and the sovereign liberty with language taken by Humpty Dumpty, he railed against what he took to be the stultification of Freud's text at the hands of post-Freudian analysts (especially in the area of ego psychology). This activity earned him an excommunication from the International Psychoanalytic Association by 1963. But he went on to found his own school where he never let people forget that Freud's discovery was the unconscious as a field of linguistic and scientific (and thereby materialist) investigation. As a matter of fact, Lacan claimed to be reading the unconscious of Freud's text—what Freud unconsciously was led to repress in his own writings. (For an account of the Freudian school of Paris [*Ecole Freudienne de Paris*] and the schisms within the French psychoanalytic movement, see Turkle, 1978.)

This view that a text might have an unconscious, a silent area that could be brought to light by textual analysis, became a model for certain Marxist critics interested in how ideology works in a text, notably Louis Althusser and, to a lesser extent, Fredric Jameson (1976). (See, for example, Althusser and Balibar, 1970, which states that "only a symptomatic reading (*lecture symptomale*) constructing the problematic, the unconscious of the text, is a reading of Marx's work that will allow us to establish the epistemological break that makes possible historical materialism as a science," 317.)

As the Marxists were quick to see, the theory of textuality, whatever fundamental objections may be made to it, has at least the advantage as a strategy of obliging the reader to give an account of his/her object of study qua text. The reader is thus no longer tempted to view it as some kind of empirically existing reality in its own right (Richards's insistence on finding the "threads" of a poem's texture that guide our response is a rough equivalent to this). Likewise in his own copious theoretical writings, the *Ecrits* (1977a), Lacan goes directly to the site of the unconscious kept to by Freud: the discourse of the subject reported to the analyst during the analytic session.

Lacan devotes much of his attention to Freud's many remarks on the irruptive nature of the unconscious as it manifests itself in language jokes, slips of the tongue, and dreams, all of which can be said to go against the conscious intentions of the ego. To quote two well-known aphorisms from this book: Lacan insists that the Freudian unconscious is "structured as a language," and that in this unconscious "man's desire is the desire of the Other," the Other being defined as the locus from which language, the bearer of symbolic social codes, operates. In order to express our desires we must of necessity enter into the alienating realm of the symbolic. Both phrases are intended to remind us that the unconscious can be understood only through the symbolic functions of the word, and through the analysis of texts, whether in the form of a dream report (which is not, I hasten to add, the dream itself as an experience of the imaginary) or other linguistic documents.

In his *Ecrits*, Lacan demonstrated also his verve in using literature (the *Ecrits* opens with the famous seminar on Poe's short story, "The Purloined Letter," which at the very least is ramifying allegory of the analytic process). But in his seminars in particular, Lacan's aim seems to have been to effect a kind of analytic listening. By means of a brilliant and often hermetic literary style (called "paranoid" by even his most ardent admirers) replete with puns, literary allusions, and syntactic aporias, Lacan exposed his audience and himself to the radical decentering effects (to what Freud called "His Majesty The Ego") of the unconscious field. Many intellectuals have written accounts of what it was like to attend one of these seminars, especially women intellectuals who sensed that Lacan had something important to say to them (in fact, some claim that his thinking is based entirely on the study of female paranoia).

Catherine Clement, a former pupil and disciple of Lacan who regularly attended the seminar in Paris, claims that Lacan used the most powerful elements of the paranoid style—the incommunicable strangeness of the delirious text—with calculated effect:

> I say again, with calculated effect. For invariably, along with the hermetic phrases, he slipped in a limpid sentence or two. Just when the meaning seemed most obscure there would glimmer a flash of logic that made it possible to put all of the pieces together. Still, he took from his familiarity with paranoid inspiration his knowledge of a dangerous and subtle game; he walked the fine line between communication and noncommunication, between light and darkness: the *midire*, or mid-speak, the art of the half-spoken thought. [Clement, 1983: 59]

Thus while explicating Freud, whose most paranoid statement was perhaps that the ego is not master in its own house, Lacan operated with a dialectic of language that was both open and closed. Lacan tried to simulate the language of the delirious subject, which is closed and deliberately selective. But in trying to do so he thereby put his audience in the position of a psychoanalyst who must listen in silence but finally "open" or interpret a text. He believed that this kind of speech—or the transcript of his seminars—would reveal more of the nature of the unconscious field in culture than any straightforward presentation in logical discourse of Freud's metapsychology (remember that I mentioned at the outset of this paper that the theory of the text is suspicious of any metalanguage).

Judging from the reception of Freud's dream theory alone, we would have to say that Lacan's approach to the "truth" of Freud's text, if somewhat circuitous, has justification. Freud, whose own style was the lucid antithesis of Lacan's, complained in his *New Introductory Lectures on Psychoanalysis* (1965) that despite all his efforts to clarify the theory of dreams, scientists, literary men, and the public at large still did not comprehend his discovery. Ironically, Freud said, he was in a position to claim this because in the thirty years since the publication of *The Interpretation of Dreams* (1900) he had received "innumerable letters" from those who claimed to have read his book, letters asking for information about the nature of dreams, and presenting him with dreams for interpretation, letters that betrayed their lack of understanding in every sentence. In others words, Freud realized belatedly that the problem in communicating his theory of the dream was that his method of dealing with the text of a dream was indeed a curious affair, "not the usual way of dealing with a communication or utterance" (Freud, 1965: 7–8).

From the character of Freud's remarks it is reasonable to assert that he was dealing with a difficulty in reading that Richards called the stock response (though there certainly may have been others, such as difficulties with imagery, and mnemonic irrelevancies). Stock responses have their opportunity, according to Richards, whenever a text involves views and emotions already fully prepared in the reader's mind; we are blocked from a full response to the text (Richards, 1963: 223–40). Especially revealing are those responses that included dreams for Freud to interpret, as if there were some symbolic code or "master key" that Freud knew would unlock the secrets of dream images as in traditional books of dream interpretation and mysticism. The irony of the situation was that Freud claimed that his dream theory ("what is most characteristic and peculiar about the young science") had uncovered a stretch of new country reclaimed from popular beliefs and mysticism, but despite all his efforts his readers—scientists, literary men, and the public at large—still did not comprehend his discovery. What they were missing, I would say, is the experience of textuality. For Freud's interpretive strategy with the dream was a textual process built largely upon the patient's personal associations and not upon any symbology (unlike Jung's theory of the dream).

Freud was writing at almost the same time as Richards, and like Richards, he still had faith in the dream of communication (if not the communication of the dream). Lacan, on the other hand, sees the difficulties of communicating Freud's interpretation of dreams as much more problematic, as not simply a matter of removing certain technical faults in the communication process. There is no room here for anything like an adequate account of Lacanian psychoanalysis. Analyzing a brief passage from one of Lacan's seminars dealing with the theory of dreams might, however, give us some insight into a problem that Richards thought was at the root of a lot of misreading: the problem of narcissism, a "very frequent cause of erratic reading" (Richards, 1963: 237).

In a seminar given in February 1964, Lacan discussed the role of imagery in the dream, weaving a text that was full of puns and enigmatic allusions to the works of Freud and those of an ancient Chinese mystic, Chuang-tsu. Like Freud, he was anxious to distinguish the Freudian "scientific" view of the dream from that of the mystic about whom he is at times very ironic. Nonetheless, he seems to have drawn his poetic inspiration from the visionary qualities of Chuang-tsu's butterfly dream and comes off himself as something of a shaman guiding us through a dream experience. I will come to this passage in a moment, but first a brief account of the origins of narcissism according to Lacan is necessary.

That the ego has a capacity to fail to recognize (*méconnaissance*) was the very foundation of his technique of analysis. In his famous essay "The Mirror Stage," Lacan argued that the image in the mirror seen at any early stage of development by the child becomes the prototype for all later images of the self. This represents for the child, for the first time, the image of itself as a unified, controllable body that is visible to others. The child greets this image with an expression of jubilation. The mirror stage is, however, no cause for jubilation, for the child fatally takes this specular image to be real, his/her real self. It is an unconscious, alienated image that will govern the child's relations with other children in the dialectics of intersubjectivity and it begins also a kind of internal rivalry in the child. So, subjects become aware of their desire in the other, through the intermediary of the image of the other, which offers them the semblance of their own mastery.

It is this notion of a specular ego, which is particularly visible in dreams, that perception generates. In one way or another, Freud said, every image in the dream is about the person dreaming. Lacan modifies this by saying that it is not the sleeper but the other to whom the dream is addressed. Or, a bit more precisely, the images of the dream presuppose an unconscious Other to whom they are addressed and to whom they display themselves. That is why, in his punning phrase, *ça montre*, "it [the Freudian id, *le ça*] shows." The dreamer's narcissistic desire is therefore the desire of the Other, for he sees himself as an object, an ego, in the eyes of the Other. In a dream we may also have the uneasy experience of *le regard* (the gaze)—objects may appear to be looking at us, displaying themselves for us. The experience can only be one of a trap, a lure, which, Lacan says in a provocative phrase, "situates the agency of the ego, before its social determination, in a fictional direction" (Lacan, 1977a: 2).

Enough has now been said for us to examine a segment of Lacan's style from the seminar. Throughout the passage, Lacan is trying to evoke the exchange that takes place between the subject's image and the image of the other in the dream:

> When Chuang-tsu wakes up, he may ask himself whether it is not the butterfly who dreams that he is Chuang-tsu. Indeed he is right, and doubly so, first because it proves he is not mad, he does not regard himself as absolutely identical with Chuang-tsu and, secondly, because he does not fully understand how right he is. In fact it is when he was the butterfly [i.e., when he was dreaming] that he apprehended one of the roots of his identity—that he was, and is, in his essence (*dans son essence*) that butterfly who paints himself with his own colors—and it is because of this that, in the last resort, he is Chuang-tsu. [Lacan, 1977b: 76]

If one of the fundamental techniques of ambiguity is to give a single word opposite and contradictory meanings (as Empson [1930/1978] so ably demonstrated), one of which is known only to those who are in the know, then Lacan surely is carrying on with his "mid-speak," his paranoid style, in this passage, which is both open and closed: closed to those who have not read his theories on the mirror stage, and open to the ears of the chosen few, his disciples and friends, who have come to hear the persecuted prophet deliver his message. He seems to be saying to them that it is at the heart of the mirage of the dream that we have to search, in the person who plays the leading role, for the sleeper's own person *à ses propres couleurs*, in his own colors (Lacan is hinting at the intensification of color in the dream, part of the dream's attempt to mislead us). For those in the know, the significance of Chuang-tsu's butterfly dream for Lacan is revealed in his use of the word "essence." Lacan is serious when he says that the essence of the gaze, the essence of human desire, is summed up by Chuang-tsu's butterfly dream. (The text of Chuang-tsu's butterfly dream is given in *The Complete Works of Chuang-tsu*, 1970.) Yet this is because Chuang-tsu, the famous Chinese seer capable of reflecting on his own dream experience (or rather, on the difference between waking and dreaming), "does not know how right he is" when he doubts that he is absolutely identical with Chuang-tsu (essence implies self-identity).

Lacan goes on to add that Chuang-tsu is, when awake, a captive butterfly caught in the butterfly net of others (meaning their language, their name for him, his position in the social order) because he must fashion a report of his dream by writing a text and representing himself as a butterfly. But when he is dreaming, he is a butterfly for nobody, Lacan says, captured by nothing, in fact, more than his own image. Using the text of Chuang-tsu's butterfly dream in this manner, and then by comparing it with the famous butterfly dream of the Wolf Man whom Freud analyzed, Lacan really asks us to experience the unconscious as a textual process, an exchange of metaphors and metonymies. (Concerning a semiotic account of metaphor and metonymy in the psychoanalytic process, see Bar, 1971. And Freud, 1963, for his account of the Wolf Man's phobic butterfly dream as a symbolic screen-memory, which may be his clearest analysis of the unconscious as a text. See also Elam, in this volume.)

The virtues of Lacan's "mid-speak" approach, of saying things by halves, are perhaps dubious, but then how successful was Freud at communicating his theory of dreams? Unlike Freud, Lacan resists the desire to "say it all," in some metalanguage (actually, Freud was aware of the problem and spoke of the dangers of metapsychology by personifying it as a "witch"). Rather, with his own evocative silences Lacan invites his reader to interpret the ambiguities and ironies—the difficulties—of his text, warning us at the outset, however, that what he has to say about dreams may remain enigmatic.

Although Lacan was committed to the powers of the spoken word, in his seminars examining the nature of textuality in Freud he was the first to introduce the notion of the text as a chain of signifiers. He seems to invite us, starting from the text itself, to find its "true" meaning where the sliding of the signifier would ultimately rest in a stable signified or "message." Of course this "true" meaning would exist nowhere but in the text and would be found in the gaps of the text, in its strange lapses, which interpretation would fill in. In his early writings Lacan instructs us to follow the letter of Freud's text and to ironize any critical preconception we may have toward Freud as a popular image. But irony in Lacan does not always make the incoherent in Freud meaningful (this is really a New Critical assumption about its function). More often than not, irony in Lacan, such as we have seen above, undoes meaning by producing uncertainty. Freud had said that a dream does not want to say anything to anyone; it is not a vehicle for communication, it is meant to remain ununderstood. The implication is that like dreams, literary texts such as Chuang-tsu's butterfly dream, do not speak and their final aim is not communication. Like dreams also, they seek to conceal their meaning to a certain extent. But nonetheless, because they both (or at least the dream report) use writing and a specific kind of representation Freud investigated, to an extent they must remain comprehensible. Literary texts are, in short, double texts, a notion I will explore with Jacques Derrida.

Lacan's writings really mark the end of—or at least an epistemological break with—naive reading in French criticism, of the sort I. A. Richards analyzed so well in his *Practical Criticism*. They also mark the birth of an unflagging attention to what in a text (bits of nonsense, lacunas) resists intelligibility. For his part, Richards had excoriated "message" theories of reading, which argue the value of a literary text on the presence or absence of "inspiring thoughts" to be gotten out of it. As a matter of fact he argued that the readers' quest for a message could blind them to the differences of the literary text (also, by implication, difference from itself; the literary text may not be self-identical): "Value in poetry turns nearly always upon differences and connections too minute and unobtrusive to be directly perceived" (p. 284). He was suspicious of most critical keywords, because they excelled in duplicity. Richards wanted to instill in readers a "virulent culture of doubt" so that all critical certainties (except one: the belief in meaning) would wither in their minds. Lacan on the other hand gives us elusive, yet resonant key terms—*midire, l'objet petit a, le regard*—but his ironies are directed against those who would use them to find an inspirational message in dreams such as Chuang-tsu's butterfly dream.

Unlike Lacan, Richards did not possess a self-consciously articulated theory of the text, though he did operate with a four-part theory of meaning, which he thought necessary to grasp the complexities of meaning in the literary text. In his later writings, however, we may observe a shift in his thinking away from positivism and toward hermeneutics. In *Coleridge on Imagination* (1935), for example, we see him arguing that the meaning of a "difficult" poem may be indefinitely postponed. A poem such as T. S. Eliot's "Ash Wednesday," Richards argues, "will come into being for very few readers without movements of exploration and resultant ponderings.... And yet these very movements—untrackable as they perhaps are, and uninducible as they almost certainly are by any other words—are the life of the poem. In these searchings for meanings *of a certain sort* [my emphasis] its being consists" (p. 216).

Richards goes on to dispute a passage of Eliot's about the supposed difficulty of modern poetry, because Eliot in his view is not precise enough about the sorts of meanings that readers expect to find in poetry. It turns out that difficulty for Richards derives from differences between the actual structures of the meanings of the poetry and the structures that are *supposed* to be natural and necessary to it. Lacan's writings, on the other hand, grant great authority to the texts of Freud because of his ability to track the disruptive effects of the unconscious in language (puns, slips of the tongue, jokes). The scandal of Lacan to most readers, though, is that he ultimately grants little authority to meaning: our conscious lives are "textualized" by the "letter" of the unconscious, by bits of unconscious nonsense. Like a true structuralist, he shows meaning arising out of the play of nonmeaning. Metaphor, a topic I will take up in the next section, is for Lacan "located precisely at the point where meaning is produced out of non-meaning" (1977a: 158). Richards may have been willing to defer meaning, but he would not have made metaphor part of a chain of repressed signifiers. Richards believed in the dream of communications, Lacan in the (always enigmatic) communication of the dream.

JACQUES DERRIDA AND METAPHOR IN THE TEXT OF PHILOSOPHY

One of the prominent sources of difficulty in reading discussed by Richards was figurative language. Many readers in the protocols simply could not distinguish metaphor from literal statement, and thus they fell into the trap of "overliteral" reading (p. 184). At the time of his *Practical Criticism*, Richards wondered how he was to explain to those who saw nothing but a tissue of ridiculous exaggerations in poetical language, what way the sense of metaphor was to be read. He gave us his theory of metaphor in *The Philosophy of Rhetoric* (1936). In this book, Richards expounded what might seem an uncompromising line on the central importance of metaphor. "Thought is metaphoric," Richards declared, "and the metaphors of language derive therefrom" (p. 94). Furthermore, Richards argued that traditional studies of metaphor (which argued that figures are a mere embellishment or added beauty, and that the plain meaning, the tenor, is what alone really matters and is something that, regardless of the figures, might be gathered by the patient reader) were not very profitable. Richards had encountered too many misreadings to believe that this "classical" theory would be of much help.

A modern theory of metaphor would object, according to Richards, that in many of the most important uses of metaphor, the co-presence of the vehicle and the tenor results in a meaning (which Richards wants clearly distinguished from the tenor) that is not attainable without their interaction in a text. As Christopher Norris points out, in contesting the traditional view of metaphor, and reversing an entrenched priority (the view that literal meaning is what we want to arrive at in reading metaphor, which is merely an incidental supplement of language), Richards goes some way toward the deconstructionist outlook of Jacques Derrida (Norris, 1982: 58–59). As a matter of fact, Derrida cites Richards with approval in his study of metaphor, "The White Mythology" (Derrida, 1982: 228). For Derrida, Richards's theory with its distinction between metaphorical tenor and metaphorical vehicle (in which sense the meaning must clearly be distinguished from the tenor) is useful because it problematizes and delays our quest for a literal ground. But Derrida parts company with Richards and his belief that a theory of metaphor or logical metalanguage could be devised that would allow us to step outside the figural domain.

Derrida's argument in "The White Mythology" is tightly woven, and I can deal with it here only in summary fashion. By a very close study of so-called worn-out or dead metaphors in philosophical texts from Aristotle to Hegel, Nietzsche and Heidegger, the paradox Derrida traces is this: there is no discourse on metaphor that is not stated within a metaphorically engendered conceptual network. There is no non-metaphorical standpoint from which to perceive the order and the demarcation of the metaphorical field. Metaphor is metaphorically stated. Furthermore, the theory of metaphor returns in a circular manner to the metaphor of theory, which determines in the whole history of Western philosophy the truth of being in terms of presence. The effort to decipher figures in philosophical texts is self-defeating: metaphor is not just a block to the communication of the concept that could be "deobstructed" by some theory of meaning in the mode of Richards; its effects are absolutely uncontrollable (for a good summary of Derrida's argument, to which this summary is indebted, see Ricoeur, 1977). To take one example that Derrida uses, in the very theory of metaphor we find the hierarchical opposition of meaning to its metaphorical signifier, without taking into account that the separation between sense (the signified) and the senses (sensory signifier) is enunciated by means of the same root (*sensus, Sinn*), permitting to be called *sense* that which should be foreign to the senses (Derrida, 1982: 228).

Metaphor doubles and endangers the philosophical text. It is determined by philosophy as a provisional loss of meaning, "an economy of the proper without irreparable damage, a certainly inevitable detour, but also a history with its sights set on, and within the horizons of, the circular reappropriation of literal, proper meaning" (p. 210). Derrida's deconstructive attempt in this essay is to explode the reassuring opposition of the metaphoric and the proper, to write another self-destruction of metaphor that doubles the philosophical one to the point of being taken for it, because it resembles it. But Derrida is saying this doubleness is an aspect of all texts, not just philosophical ones. For Derrida, every text is a double text, there are always two texts in one: "Two texts, two hands, two visions, two ways of listening. Together simultaneously and separately" (p. 65). The reading of the text therefore requires a "double science" (*la double séance*), rendering apparent the duplicity of any text (see "The Double Session" in Derrida's *Dissemination*, 1981).

According to Vincent Descombes, convention has us picture meta-physics as splitting the world into two, into the sensible and the intelligi-ble, the body and the soul, tenor and vehicle (most summary treatments of Richards's theory of metaphor tend to be a lot more binary and "meta-physical" than his own text suggests, and Derrida shows). And philo-sophical empiricism (in which we can probably include the I. A. Richards of *Practical Criticism*), in a protest no less classic, overthrew this Platon-ism, and maintained that the intelligible arises from the sensible, that thought is a faculty of the body, and so forth. But Derrida's double sci-ence, "by an unprecedented operation, splits the metaphysical text itself into two. It is the text's duplicity which enables the manifest text to 'exceed' or 'transgress' in the direction of the latent text (to use by approximation, an analogy from Freudian dream theory)" (Descombes, 1980: 151).

Thus it is by means of demonstrating the duplicity of texts them-selves that the Derridean theory of the text is literally justified. More closely than Lacan, Derrida devotes himself to the letter of the text. And if writing—literal writing—has up to now been treated as a mere supple-ment (the argument in *Of Grammatology*) to speech, Derrida will turn the scapegoating of writing around and insist on a rigorous literalism of the text in which it appears that writing is the name metaphorically attached to whatever eludes, subverts, or opposes the discourse of logocentric rea-son. (I might mention here what theorists of the text often point out, that "text" itself is a metaphor derived from the Latin *textus*, meaning "woven." For a lucid discussion of how "literal" reading operates in deconstruction, see Norris, 1987. My account here is a compressed ver-sion of that given by Norris.)

Unfortunately, space does not allow me to discuss Derrida's project in *Of Grammatology* (but see Hazard Adams, in this volume, on the histor-ical opposition between literal writing and allegorical or spiritual truth), nor his remarks on paraphrase (Derrida, 1982: 40–46), but I should men-tion what is important to remember about deconstruction with regard to the notion of difficulty. As Jonathan Culler indicates, deconstruction is not a theory that defines meaning in order to tell you how to find it. Rather, "As a critical undoing of the hierarchical oppositions on which theories depend, it *demonstrates the difficulties* [my emphasis] of any theory that would define meaning in an univocal way: as what an author intends, what conventions determine, what a reader experiences" (Culler, 1982: 131). I interpret this observation strongly, in the sense that deconstruc-tion itself can be read as a theory of difficulty. Richards had argued that intellectual tradition tells us *literally* how to read: "It guides us in our metaphorical, allegorical, symbolical modes of interpretation" (Richards, 1935: 193). But Derrida replaces this hermeneutic authority of tradition with the notion of the general text (*le texte général*), which has no bound-aries. So the "text of philosophy" in Derrida's reading is part of this gen-eral text in which it is difficult to locate where meaning resides (though we may wish to make determinations of meaning for pragmatic reasons, as Culler points out).

The implications of Derrida's views on metaphor are not only that concepts are not separable in their adequacy or inadequacy from metaphors—a point made by Richards and echoed by Derrida—but also that the very notions of what in a text might be nonmetaphorical are con-cepts whose force owes much to their figural attractions (one would have to consider here the effect on reading of rhetorical figures; see Elam, in this volume, or the writings of Paul de Man).

Interestingly enough in view of the difficulties involved in reading philosophical texts, Derrida is closely involved in France with GREPH (Groupe de Recherches sur l'Enseignement Philosophique), a collective set up to examine the various ways in which philosophy has been taught in the French school and university system. Acting as a kind of philo-sophical interest group, GREPH has demanded an extension of the number of hours of philosophy taught in the French school system, but above all it wishes to defend the *"classe de philosophie"*—the teaching of philosophy in the final year of the *lycée*, against those who would argue that it is too "difficult" a subject to teach there. (For an account of the activities and publications of GREPH, see Fynsk, 1978.)

ROLAND BARTHES AND THE PLEASURE OF THE TEXT

Another area of difficulty in reading that Richards distinguished—and which Barthes was preoccupied with in his later writings—was not concept formation but the function of images in reading. Some readers in Richards's protocols were definitely operating with an imagistic theory of meaning, which Richards was at some pains to refute. Indeed, so con-cerned was he about it that he devoted a special appendix to arguing that it is also possible to think concretely without any imagery of any kind. Confusion and prejudice on this point were chiefly due, Richards said, to a too simple idea of what is necessary for mental representation. Richards (1963) points out that an image (insofar as it represents by being a copy) can only represent things that are like one another, but a word is "a point at which very different influences may cross and unite" (p. 344). For the very reason that a word is not like its meaning, it can represent an enor-mously wide range of different things.

It is this respect for the *differences* of meaning that gives Richards's writings something of a contemporary flavor. But still, Richards was pre-occupied with a theory of meaning and not with a theory of the text. For his part, Barthes is very clear about the fact that theory of the text is constituted by a withdrawal from the image-systems of language: "The text is language without its image-reservoir, its image-system" (Barthes, 1975: 33). As pointed out in the passage from Barthes cited in the introduction of this paper, the pedagogical problem as Barthes saw it was to make adolescents understand that there is text everywhere, but that not everything is text. Writing (*écriture*, as opposed to *écrivance*, the unselfconscious writing of discourses) was the type of practice that would allow us to dissolve the image-repertoires of our language. "Image-repertoire" is a term coined by Barthes with which he designates the Lacanian imaginary—a set of images functioning as a misunderstanding of the subject by itself. As such, it is critical of narcissistic reading.

In narcissistic reading (which Richards characterized so well), the reader is cut off from any relation to the world of production, and he projects only his own psychology: "The reader who cannot write projects his image-repertoire (the narcissistic zone of the psyche), very far from his muscular, carnal body, the body of *jouissance*. He is drawn into the trap of the image-repertoire" (Barthes, 1985: 241). However, Barthes also made it clear that one cannot write *without* the image-repertoire. Barthes realized that he had a vital relation to past literature precisely because that literature provided him with a good relation to images (or as he puts it in his own parlance, he "recognized himself" there as the subject of an image-repertoire). As for the text, it could only be a braid, woven in an extremely twisted and devious fashion between the symbolic field of language and the image-repertoire. That is to say, in the process of writing as Barthes conceives of it, the image-repertoire would be undone in a kind of back-and-forth movement between the Lacanian registers of the imaginary and the symbolic.

Evidently, Barthes had no use for the Lacanian register of the Real, unless it could be the body. Perhaps the most interesting thing about Barthes as a critic was his insistence in his later writings on the pleasures of the text, which are always plural and bodily. He distinguishes between pleasure (*plaisir*), which is linked to a consistence of the self, of the subject, which is assured in values of comfort, relaxation, ease—for Barthes it was the entire realm of reading the classics—and bliss (*jouissance*), the system of reading, or utterance, through which the subject, instead of establishing itself, is lost.

The great majority of texts we know and love consist roughly of texts of pleasure, while texts of bliss are, according to Barthes, extremely rare, primarily because of the historical and institutional tendency of reading in culture to recuperate any loss of meaning. And there is no assurance given by Barthes that bliss could be made a part of any historical curriculum, or that it would be possible to root out entirely the process of adhering to an image in a movement of identification that accompanies much of the activity of "passive" reading in modern consumer society (see Lasch, 1979, for a recent investigation of the effects of mass culture). Yet he did not entirely despair.

Is it still possible to learn how to read in schools? Barthes gives us a qualified yes as an answer to this weighty question, providing that the function of institutional codes is clearly identified, and the accomplishments of liberal secular schooling are maintained, but redirected toward the exercise of *l'esprit critique*, the decipherment of codes, supported by semiological studies. In the type of writing/reading Barthes inaugurated in his critical works such as the *S/Z* (1974), we get a glimpse of this transmuted practice. It would be one in which we would turn ourselves into psychoanalytical subjects by writing. We would conduct a transferential analysis on ourselves, recognize our "I" and its complicity with an image-repertoire. At this point, presumably, the relationship between subject and object would be playfully displaced, as it is in Lacan's intertextual "reading" of Chuang-tsu's butterfly dream. Only in this way, thought Barthes, could we reinvent the ideological necessity to represent ourselves, which inhabits all language.

We may conclude this investigation into the theory of the text with the observation that the old opposition between subjectivity as an attribute of impressionistic criticism (what Richards sought to defend students against with better techniques of reading) and objectivity as an attribute of scientific criticism (Richards's dream of communication, or the early Barthes) becomes in the last analysis unimportant. Barthes remarks that traditionally schools have taught something on the order of doubt or truth—an alternative difficult to escape. But with the theory of the text as writing, as an indefinite field in permanent metamorphosis, where language is ceaselessly at play weaving our culture's social codes, Barthes believed that we could institute a process of liberation in which meaning would not "pass through a return of the signified." Students would then experience meaning not so much as an effect of power, mastery, or appropriation, but as the result of a patient and passionate weaving and unweaving: "There would be a whole spectrum of projects, tasks that would be directed roughly toward a *disappropriation* of the text" (Barthes, 1985: 149). And finally, with regard to the role of teachers: "We must not teach skepticism but doubt bolstered by *jouissance*" (p. 242).

ACKNOWLEDGMENTS

I am grateful to Jonathan Culler for pointing out to me certain activities of GREPH of which I was unaware. Also, I should mention that certain notions in Culler's *Framing the Sign: Criticism and its Institutions* (1988) have been useful to me. What Culler says about de Man—that he grants great authority to texts but very little to meaning (p. 131)—is, I think, to a large extent true of all three of the French thinkers I have considered here. Certainly Lacan is always pointing out the difficulty of reading his texts: "[the text] makes possible the kind of tightening up that I like in order to leave the reader no other way out than the way in, which I prefer to be difficult" (Lacan, 1977a: 146), or "Do we say this in order to explain the difficulty of the desire? No, rather to say that the desire is constituted by difficulty" (p. 268).

REFERENCES

Althusser, L., and Balibar, E. (1970). *Reading capital.* London: New Left Books.

Bakhtin, M. (1986). *Speech genres and other late essays* (V. McGee, trans.). Austin: University of Texas Press.

Bar, E. (1971). "The language of the unconscious according to Jacques Lacan." *Semiotica*, 3: 241–68.

Barthes, R. (1974). *S/Z* (R. Miller, trans.). New York: Hill and Wang.

———. (1975). *The pleasure of the text* (R. Miller, trans.). New York: Hill and Wang.

———. (1981). "The theory of the text." In R. Young, ed., *Untying the text: A post-structuralist reader.* London: Routledge and Kegan Paul.

———. (1985). *The grain of the voice* (L. Coverdale, trans.). New York: Hill and Wang.

Chuang-tsu (1970). *The complete works of Chuang-tsu* (B. Watson, trans.). New York: Columbia University Press.

Clement, C. (1983). *The lives and legends of Jacques Lacan* (A. Goldhammer, trans.). New York: Columbia University Press.

Culler, J. (1982). *On deconstruction.* Ithaca: Cornell University Press.

———. (1988). *Framing the sign: Criticism and its institutions.* Norman: University of Olkahoma Press.

Decombes, V. (1980). *Modern French philosphy* (L. Scott-Fox and J. M. Harding, trans.). Cambridge: Cambridge University Press.

———. (1981). *Dissemination.* B. Johnson, trans.). Chicago: University of Chicago Press.

————. (1982). *Margins of philosophy* (A. Bass, trans.). Chicago: University of Chicago Press.

Derrida, J. (1976). *Of grammatology* (G. Spivak, trans.). Baltimore: Johns Hopkins University Press.

Empson, W. (1978). *Seven types of ambiguity.* New York: New Directions. (Originally published 1930)

Freud, S. (1963). "The wolf man." In Rieff, ed., *Three case histories* (J. Strachey, trans.). New York: Collier Books.

————. *New introductory lectures on psychoanalysis* (J. Strachey, trans. and ed.). New York: W. W. Norton.

Freund, E. (1987). *The return of the reader.* New York: Methuen.

Fynsk, C. I. (1978). "A decelebration of philosophy." *Diacritics,* 8 (2), (Summer): 80–90.

Hartman, G. (1975). *The fate of reading.* Chicago: University of Chicago Press.

Hertz, N. (1985). "The notion of blockage in the literature of the sublime." In G. Hartman, ed., *Psychoanalysis and the question of the text.* Baltimore: Johns Hopkins University Press.

Jameson, F. (1976). The ideology of the text. *Salmagundi,* 31–32, (Fall–Winter): 204–46.

Kristeva, J. (1980). *Desire in language: A semiotic approach to literature and art* (L. S. Roudiex et al., trans.). New York: Columbia University Press.

Lacan, J. (1977a). *Ecrits: A selection* (A. Sheridan, trans.). New York: W. W. Norton.

Lacan, J. (1977b). *The four fundamental conceits of psychoanalysis* (A. Sheridan, trans.). London: Penguin Books.

Lasch, C. (1979). *The culture of narcissism.* New York: Warner Books.

Lawall, S. (1968). *Critics of consciousness.* Cambridge: Harvard University Press.

Norris, C. (1982). *Deconstruction: Theory and practice.* London: Methuen.

————. (1987). *Derrida.* Cambridge: Harvard University Press.

Purves, A., and Beach, R. (1972). *Literature and the reader.* Urbana, Ill: NCTE Committee on Publications.

Richards, I. A. (1935). *Coleridge on imagination.* New York: Harcourt, Brace.

———. (1936). *The philosophy of rhetoric.* Oxford: Oxford University Press.

———. (1963). *Practical criticism.* New York: Harcourt, Brace. (Originally published 1929)

Ricoeur, (1977). *The rule of metaphor.* Toronto: University of Toronto Press.

Scholes, R. (1985). *Textual power.* New Haven: Yale University Press.

Turkle, S. (1978). *Psychoanalytic politics, Freud's French revolution.* New York: Basic Books.

Ulmer, G. L. (1985). *Applied grammatology.* Baltimore: Johns Hopkins University Press.

4.

The Difficulty of Reading

Helen Regueiro Elam

American culture does not take well to the idea of difficulty. Our penchant is for one-step, one-stop solutions to problems, and we expect and demand in all areas of life, including reading, an ease of achievement that is antithetical to thought itself. Newspaper ads speak of special pills for those who want to lose weight without exercising or changing their eating habits. Language programs teach "how to" speak a language in a few easy lessons. Products are either fixable or disposable, and even mental disorders are perceived in terms of therapeutic closure or cure. Difficulty is there to be overcome, disposed of, certainly not to become the invisible partner of our daily lives. An episode of Adams's *Hitchhiker's Guide to the Galaxy* captures well this movement toward answers, solutions, the transcendence of the problem. A supercomputer is asked to come up with "the meaning of life, the universe, and everything." Seven million years later, the supercomputer comes up with an answer: "42." The quest for solutions is synonymous with a reductiveness that leaves aside the problematic movement of thought. Students often tackle "education" as if it were a puzzle to be considered solved when every piece is in place. But an education—or reading—worthy of its name will recognize that when the puzzle is finally put together into a perfect whole, there is always one piece left over which forces us to rethink the edifice we have erected.

The connection of the concept of difficulty with thought itself, and therefore with the very activity of reading, goes back several centuries. Heidegger makes the connection when he refers to "the difficult work of thought" (Hartman, 1987: 198), but Plato in several of his dialogues contends with this very issue. The *Theaetetus* tackles a crucial question for philosophy: What is knowledge and how is it that we know? By the end of the dialogue, Socrates, who has been proclaiming his role as "midwife" and his capacity to separate the true from the false, recognizes that in the question of knowledge we cannot separate what we know from how we know, and that there exists, therefore, in all of us, "a depth of darkness." The dialogue thus does not move from a starting point of "not-knowing" to an end-point of "knowing." Over the issue of knowledge the *Theaetetus* truncates itself, denies itself closure or transcendence, and reaffirms the insoluble difficulty of reading. Philosophy over the centuries has aimed at an absolute, solid ground from which it could speak. But the *Theaetetus* already disperses this elegant hope. If what we know is contaminated by (implicated in) how we know, then we have no privileged point from which to view the object of discussion, and thus no claim to objectivity or to telling the true from the false. Plato's dialogue teaches us that we do not know what we know, and more troubling yet, we do not know what we do not know. Centuries later, Nietzsche will call truths "illusions of which we have forgotten that they are illusions" (Nietzsche, 1964: 180), and Freud will recognize, like Plato, our radical otherness to ourselves, the ultimate unreadability of our psyches.

In the American grain, a fair question would be—what do philosophy and psychoanalysis have to do with reading? The question of reading in America has been relegated to departments of English and schools of education, with the result that "reading" has been associated with "literacy" in its narrow definition, the definition that precisely bypasses the question of difficulty. Literacy, in its philological relation to "literature," means, of course, how to read, but also "how to read." And on the issue of reading in the profounder sense American education has been thoroughly resistant to change.

Two reasons for this resistance stand out. One is the idea that anything difficult is elitist, that democracy demands simplicity. This is a particularly pernicious notion to a country and a culture. At the political level, it means that issues and problems have to be reduced to the lowest common denominator; at the university level, it results in an anti-intellectual attitude that makes a mockery of the idea of education. Last year a graduate student auditing several undergraduate courses as part of a pedagogical project commented to me that he had problems with tough grading because such a policy perpetuates a system where the more socially and economically advantaged students receive the higher grades. The sentiment is admirable, yet lowering the level of difficulty in a class so that all grades might be high is hardly the answer to the issues of mass education. A better answer might be to widen the question of reading so that reading encompasses not just the encounter with the printed word but "life, the universe, and everything"—so that the difficulty of thought touches the students' own lives and makes that difficulty accessible to them.

A second reason for the resistance to "difficulty" is that difficulty in the practice of reading has by and large arisen out of "alien" disciplines—philosophy and psychoanalysis in particular—and American education, until the last few years, and for several decades, had been severely compartmentalized. Philosophical writings were the province of philosophy, history belonged to history, and so on. One effect of this compartmentalizing has been that individual departments have come to perceive their own disciplines as a "science," eschewing the kinds of interdisciplinary relations that would precisely put into question (render "difficult") the solid and absolute ground upon which the discipline perceives itself coming to rest. When the *Theaetetus* suggests that we cannot know anything apart from the act of knowing, it gives the lie to the scientific ground of any discipline: it underscores the rhetorical basis of all knowledge. This may be why the *Theaetetus* is not often taught in philosophy departments. Nietzsche says we can define a discipline in terms of what it forbids its practitioners to do, and that suppression has invariably been a suppression of the problematic, of the difficult, of the unstable. It has been a suppression of "reading" itself.

Surprisingly, this suppression is often actively pursued in literature departments, where texts are at times understood to be representations of experience or culture, and criticism to be a matter of "approaches" or "methods." While it would be foolish to suggest that texts have nothing to do with culture and experience, the direct and unproblematic linking of the two bypasses the act of reading. If a text is said to be a representation of culture, or individual experience, then the assumption is that language is a transparent element, that it communicates without altering, that it reflects but does not constitute the object of discussion. At the high school level, but also, often, at the college level, this assumption goes without saying. The moment character, or plot, or description are brought to rest on an external given, on a stable and determinable context, the text as such disappears—it is truly rendered transparent and invisible because all its density, all that renders it problematic or difficult, has been dispelled.

In the past, this model of mastery over the linguistic object has been true as well of relations between disciplines, and this notion of language as transparent medium has given disciplines the space to constitute themselves as a science, uncompromised by rhetoric. Thus history has been known to deal with "events" and "facts," philosophy with conceptual, abstract thought, mathematics with natural laws. Yet this "dealing with" their objects has been nothing other than a "reading" of those objects, a reading that far from being innocent and straightforward has in some measure determined and constituted those objects. Reading as representation, in all its innocence and simplicity, is superseded here by reading as interpretation, where what is known and certain and stable is dispelled under the pressure of interrogation.

This idea of reading as an interpretive, creative activity has transformed the relations between one discipline and another and has made difficult determining the boundaries between them. Philosophy figures most prominently in this new relationship, inasmuch as philosophy's quest for transcendence is based on the very notion of solid ground which reading as interpretation does away with. If some of Plato's dialogues were problematic in terms of their relationship to the concept of the absolute, Aristotle's treatises appear as a more secure, measured response—a closing off of the gaps that the Platonic dialogues open up. Over and over again Aristotle claims that the way to knowledge lies in classification and enclosure. Whether one is classifying plants or types of writing, the critical activity in Aristotle is supposedly distinct from the object of study, and thus the object of study can be read in all its facets and comprehended (in the strict sense of being surrounded on all sides). In Aristotle's metaphysics, true knowledge is possible, and it authorizes a whole range of classificatory activities designed to keep what is known in place. Nothing could make us feel more secure than to know that we know, and what we know. No depth of darkness here. Expressions of this Aristotelian metaphysics are everywhere in our culture. While buying a new car, I noticed a stunning description of its design: "Concise lines make a clear statement. They don't trouble people by disappearing here and there. The lines of the Volvo 760 GLE have a beginning and an end. They are consistent, genuine, and honest." Far more than a plug for a boxy car, this is an affirmation of form and the authority of knowledge.

Yet Aristotle is himself haunted by those disappearing lines. In the midst of his major discourse on form, *The Poetics*, he defines metaphor as the giving of a name to something to which the name does not belong. If figures of speech name wrongly—that is, if figures of speech are, precisely, "tropes," turnings from the object rather than direct representations of it—then a language constituted by such tropes will problematize the question of reading (see Derrida, 1982). Any reading that moves self-consciously into the path of these disappearing lines, that contemplates not what it knows but how it can come to know anything at all, will take us rapidly from certainty to uncertainty, from sure answers to unanswerable questions, from stable centers to disappearing lines and dislocated boundaries. If reading is a dangerous activity, this is because it has the potential to disrupt everything that we know, to make our consciousness aware of what it cannot name or encompass, in short, to make us aware of "death." This is not to detract from the power of death in all its physical manifestations, but to say that death signals above all what de Man (1984) calls "a linguistic predicament": the impossibility of transparence, the difficulty of reading (p. 81).

An entire philosophical tradition is troubled by this impossibility, but the difficulty troubles every other discipline as well and therefore affects the very structure of the university, the way in which knowledge is produced and authorized. In its most stable version, the university is a place where knowledge is imparted—a knowledge that for the most part is secure, significant, and unchangeable. But if reading is an interpretive, creative activity, then the university becomes the place where knowledge is produced, and such production is never innocent (see Culler, 1987; Godzich, 1988). The university as producer of knowledge has the power to constitute in large measure the objects of that knowledge, and this makes it important that such production be carried out as a self-conscious activity.

That self-consciousness is most often resisted, because it entails whole disciplines coming to terms with the problems of what happens when they organize themselves as disciplines, what they include and exclude, how those choices are made: in short, their "history." This is the area that Nietzsche claims a discipline forbids its practitioners to enter, so that it functions as a discipline's unconscious, something that it knows but cannot know it knows. And when such knowledge is brought to the foreground, as it has today by recent critical concerns, then the discipline undergoes a crisis. History offers a good example of this trajectory. For at least a century, historians had stressed the scientific basis of historical inquiry (the equivalent of the philosopher's absolute ground), so that the historian's account was supposed to have a solid reference point. Suppressed from this scheme was the possibility that the "event" the historian deals with might be constructed by the telling. This is not to say that historians invent their subject, or that the event as such never took place, but that we have no access to it in any original sense. Language is our access to it, and language transforms the thing it touches. What we know of an event in history is thus enfolded within the historian's story. The great historians, says Hayden White, always knew this, and built that knowledge into a rhetorical self-consciousness that distinguishes them from the rest. This foregrounding of rhetoric in relation to "content" or "reference" brings about a crisis of knowledge in historical studies (see Orr, 1986; White, 1973; 1978). What is at stake is the authority of historical narrative, and the very nature of our understanding of what we call the outside world. The concept of scientific inquiry promises solid ground, but the rhetorical status of that inquiry bears stronger links to desire than to any detached and objective knowledge. The difficulty in this respect is epistemological: what is it that we can be sure we know, in what circuitous ways do the production and the acquisition of knowledge intersect?

The epistemological issue—what is it that we can know when what we know is enfolded in rhetoric—cuts across disciplines, makes them aware of their historicity, denies them access to a totalizing, transcendent ground or the authority of what they know. To focus on the question of knowledge, on its production, is to put into question the cause and effect relations we tend to take for granted, and in turn to throw the legitimacy of what we know, of the organization of disciplines, and of the very structure of the university, into disarray. This is a far cry from Aristotelian logic, where everything, finally, has its place and stays in place, where knowledge is marked by proper beginnings and satisfying endings. Aristotle already suppresses Plato's "depth of darkness," and that suppression constitutes a sort of history of Western thought, authorizing and backing the certainties by which colonization (imaginative and geographical) can occur.

If we take colonization in its most literal meaning, as a historical and geographical appropriation, then we would have to say that American education today takes a clear stance against such zealous intrusions. Yet this avowed anticolonialist, antiestablishment stance itself constitutes another moment in that history of suppression, for it builds on the necessary assumption of certainty, the empirical dimension by which all political movements seek their goals and legitimate themselves. The very ideology that powers this certainty is deeply embedded in the suppression of that "depth of darkness," complicitous with the very structures of thought it seeks to dismantle. Political "causes" are built on a logical cause and effect relation: "this" problem is caused by "that" situation, and if we attack the cause, we will be able to rectify the problem and bring things to proper closure. What is left out of this neat paradigm is the kind of problematizing that questions, among other things, the neatness of cause and effect relations, the simplicity of the law of context, the stability of "inside" and "outside." The questioning of this relation is at once a questioning of the status quo and of the forces that seek to uproot it. To "problematize" is to bring an issue to difficulty, to raise doubts about the certainties that fuel missionary zeal. Thus the most radical questioning of the legitimacy of knowledge and of the function of the university has come not from the expected quarters—political, ideological, historical orientations—but from the persistent speculations on origins and cause and effect relations that have marked "critical theory" in the past two decades. The resistance to theory has come not only from academic departments and disciplines that insist on retaining their scientific status, but also from political constituencies demanding a cure for their marginalization. Problematization and difficulty are eschewed because they are not readily sloganizable, and because to problematize is in a very real sense to defer solution and closure, almost as if the act of problem-solving stood in opposition to genuine understanding instead of being a natural consequence of it.

Much of the history of critical theory and the history of political stances in the academy are entangled in this issue of understanding and legitimation. The literary Marxism of the 1930s (sometimes referred to as "monolithic Marxism") assumed the stability of context, of an outside given, and situated texts within those stable historical contexts. "History" itself was not placed under interrogation. Part of the impetus of the New Criticism was a response to this straightforward contextualizing of texts, to the point that texts disappeared into this outside which they were said to represent. New Criticism affirmed the in-itselfness of the work, its authority, its legitimacy, and its firm boundaries. Drawing its impetus from Aristotle's theory of form, but discarding the implications of his theory of metaphor, New Critics argued that the literary work has a meaning within its confines, and that tension, ambiguity, paradox, irony all lead to a climactic resolution. Formalism focused on the aesthetic importance of the literary object, separated it from the domain of culture and history, idealized it. The literary text appeared frozen in space, complete within itself, untouched by time or reading. It was itself its own context. And difficulty was persistently dispelled by the achieved resolution and the meaning proposed by that resolution. Formalism tended to perceive difficulty primarily embodied in elaborate and recondite allusions, but allusions were ultimately drawn into the meaning of the work at hand. They could be researched, hunted down, appropriated, held in place. On the face of it, traditional Marxism and formalism could not be further apart. Marxism historicized literature, while formalism aestheticized it. Yet formalism repeated the very gestures of the method it opposed: both engaged in a practice of offering answers, solutions, meaning, and thus in a strategy of unveiling truth and marginalizing difficulty.

This strategy is prevalent today in the persistent demand in the academy to assimilate the discourses of women and minorities—to give a voice to the oppressed and thus redress historical wrongs in the most direct, representational way. As in the case of my graduate student, the attitude is admirable, but in terms of critical theory it repeats yet once more the gestures of the patriarchal/colonialist stance it seeks to displace (see Spivak, 1989). Traditional feminist and minority approaches rely on the authority of experience and its representability in language. Experience shapes writing, and writing expresses it. Thus literature becomes the representation of culture, without either category of "literature" or "culture" being problematized, "put into question." The paradox is that representation is a profoundly conservative approach whose epistemology overlaps with that of patriarchal and colonialist discourses. The more traditional feminist and minority approaches, structured along the lines of a theory of representation, thus exhibit a strange complicity with the very power structures they oppose. The authority of these power structures depends on the invisible being made visible, and thus possessed and mastered. "The very act of rendering visible," says Sharon Willis, "expresses a capture, and a power relation" (Vickers, 1986: 34). Malek Alloula (1986) remarks on this desire for visibility in his study of a series of postcards of Algerian women during French colonization, and observes that the "brutal idiom" of the colonial postcard renders public what was until now "invisible or hidden" (p. 118). The desire for transparence and representation underwrites this particular colonialist discourse, until a whole society "ceases to be opaque, in the imaginary at least," and thus appears to have been "pacified" (p. 64). Visibility dispels that depth of darkness; it states the authority and legitimacy of possession and expresses the possibility of meaning and control. Thus both formalism and traditional feminism suppress difficulty—one by resolving it into closure, the other by supplanting it with the certainty of ideology (of "what goes without saying"). The demand for "ideology," "consensus," "commitment" may be politically correct, but it halts the movement of speculation by yielding answers that invoke the authority of empirical evidence and lived experience in the same way that the sciences invoke "scientific method." While these two models, the representation of reality and the idealization of work, appear antithetical to one another, they share a basic mistrust of interrogation that does not get to the point, and whose effect is to demystify and deauthorize the premises upon which these perspectives come to rest. Resistance to traditional power structures begins, especially in contemporary (post)feminism, as a resistance to the rhetoric of representation, of the visible, the transparent, the "clearly there," the formally contained (see Jacobus, 1986; Miller, 1986). And this resistance, in all its difficulty, finds its fullest expression in a criticism within which "theory" undermines the basic assumptions of objectivity that make knowledge possible. Difficulty opposes itself to ideology because in an ultimate sense it is synonymous with a conflict for which no solution can be posited, with a contradiction that attends every attempt at understanding. "Contradiction," says Adorno in *Negative Dialectics*, "indicates the untruth of identity, the fact that the concept does not exhaust the thing conceived" (p. 5). The remainder, or excess, is the extra piece in the completed puzzle, and as such it reopens the path of interrogation. Problematizing the issue means that solution, closure, cure are deferred, that the gap or hiatus between problem and solution cannot be bridged, that understanding is not geared to the effacement of difficulty but to a deepening, self-conscious recognition of it as an "untranscendable horizon."

There is no question that "critical theory" has been "difficult" in recent years. Part of the difficulty lies with its jargon and with its deliberate attempt to break the illusion of lucidity, the illusion that language is a transparent entity and that we are in control of it. The jargon can be mastered, and even appropriated. But the effect of this thinking was to put into question chronology, narrative, sequence, and representability— in short, our very experience of time and our sense that we know where we are and who we are at any given moment because we know who and where we have been: the ultimate expression of "representability" is "identity." If we are not in control of language, if we (and language) are haunted by a depth of darkness, then our past becomes a function of our present, an endless renarration within which identity shifts and remains infinitely elusive. Who we are may well depend on who we narrate ourselves to be, on the elaborate filiations we draw between events that are lost to us in the density of what we call experience.

The most dramatic expression of this reversal of expected cause and effect relations is brought forth in Freud's case history of the Wolf Man. There may well be other dramatic expressions, but this is the one that critical theory has focused on, so that it functions almost as a metonymy of this questioning of logical sequence and of the possibility of representative discourse. (On the Wolf Man and its implications, see Brooks, 1984; Culler, 1982; Lukacher, 1986; Warner, 1986.) In this case history, Freud tries to give a "history"; that is, to "give" a history, to unveil an etiology of the patient's neurosis, to establish that first there was this cause, and then came these effects. What results from this case history is the opposite. Having surmised that the man's neurosis stems from the child's witnessing of his parents' intercourse, Freud then recognizes that this "primal scene" does not become traumatic until years later, when another event triggers it into memory and renders it traumatic. The earlier event is logically the cause of the trauma, but the later event is just as logically the cause of the earlier event becoming traumatic. Cause and effect here are hopelessly confused, and problematized by Freud's own narrative, layered by revisions and bracketed insertions. It is impossible to locate an "origin" or cause because we are always implicated in the construction or narration of that origin or cause. Indeed, Freud goes on to suggest that the primal scene is itself a construct or "phantasy." Origins, like myths, are imagined things, and theory for Freud becomes akin to phantasy, inextricably bound to the wish, to what we want to "see." Far from narration being a cure (coming to an end), it becomes a repeated expression of the disease. When Dickinson says that we "cannot see to see" she is expressing this impossibility of getting beyond that depth of darkness. When we truly see, we see that darkness, the density that cannot be mastered, and to which we give the name of "death."

It may well be that critical theory (of the poststructuralist sort) has been overconcerned with death. But death becomes a "topic" in criticism because it stands metonymically for what is unthematizable, unrepresentable, unnameable, unteachable—and thus for an insoluble difficulty synonymous with thought itself. Death becomes another trope for contradiction, for the otherness that haunts us; it is the end that we cannot possess, and that renders all our possessions improper.

All this is "difficult" stuff, and it flies in the face of what Lyotard calls "the ideology of transparency," by which language and knowledge and learning are systematized—into composition courses, into criticism courses, into creative writing workshops, into the "proper" arrangement of knowledge, so that nothing is lost, all is recuperated into some classification, some form. The name for such arrangement is "method," and its subtext is "science." It may be in the very nature of academic institutions to formalize learning and knowledge, and thus to subscribe to this ideology of transparency. But the cost of this ideology is nothing less than thinking itself. Heidegger takes a dim view of "method" and all its formalist underpinnings: "method, especially in today's modern scientific thought, is not a mere instrument serving the sciences; rather, it has pressed the sciences into its own service." And Nietzsche is as explicit: "It is not the victory of science that distinguishes our nineteenth century, but the victory of scientific method over science" (Bruns, 1989: 110). Method in American education is today the fancy name for a "how to" approach to life and learning. It is fueled by a pragmatic desire for efficiency which privileges clarity over density and knowing where you are over wandering or allowing yourself to get lost. Thus method becomes a kind of all-encompassing cartography without a history, displacing error (and errancy) and getting "it" right. Even (especially) in the realm of theory, the most common complaint is that some critics are just "too difficult," and the demand placed on theory is that it "do its job" and clarify the whole mess of frayed thinking, giving out some decent labels and classifying (possessing) the landscape. In America at least, the demands placed on the intellectual scene are not all that different from those placed on the public sphere. Be clear—communicate. What is lost in this demand, in the Heideggerian sense, is the depth of darkness we inhabit, our homelessness, our exile, the very condition of thinking itself. "By continually appealing to the logical," says Heidegger (1977), "one conjures up the illusion that he is entering straightforwardly into thinking when in fact he has disavowed it" (p. 227). Heidegger insists on the importance of Plato's depth of darkness and intimates that thinking is a kind of lingering in the area of the unrepresentable. The difficult work of thought demands that we learn to read slowly, that we "linger," that we allow ourselves to get lost in "paths" that are not mapped. And certain strands of critical theory seem to have heeded Heidegger's call.

Thinkers like Lacan and Derrida have drawn theory into a path of speculation that specifically rejects the possibility of metatheory, of classification, clarification, understanding in the sense of seeing "the whole" from some privileged point of view. If what we know is inseparable from how we know, then theory and practice are not separable, with theory functioning as "method" and practice as the playing out of method, but both are implicated in and contaminated by one another. Far from functioning as a metalanguage, this sort of criticism points to the impossibility of any systematizing method, of any metatheory that would not already be implicated in the very problems it would seek to resolve (see Young, 1981). What emerges from this is a philosophy of the fragment, and a theoretical criticism that identifies reading with estrangement and difficulty.

For a country that places its faith in speed and efficiency—the manifestations of which run a whole gamut from speed reading courses to drive-in churches—this kind of thinking is disruptive and pointless. Our aim is always to make texts appear less strange, more accessible, assimilable to our culture and therefore more transparent—like the rewriting of the New Revised Version of the Bible. At the other end of the spectrum are poets like Hölderlin or Dickinson, who remain radically strange or estranged from us, and who beckon us into an interstice where difficulty is fully played out. Poetry inhabits a space where logic and clarity do not hold sway, where language opens up strange paths that defy all our intellectual classifications and attempts at possession. As Gerald Bruns (1989) so eloquently shows us, in such spaces we are not in control—of our language, of ourselves, of the poem and its meaning. And when we encounter this kind of "difficulty," we are at the beginning of thinking.

Just what kind of reading does a difficult poet entice us into? What consequences would a more stable reading of the same poet entail? And how do we "democratize" access to difficulty without making difficulty disappear into method? Dickinson is a good choice with which to open these questions, because she is so thoroughly resistant to method that she makes evident the limits of ideological and formalist stances. Formalist editors in the 1940s and 50s routinely substituted normal punctuation for her dashes, gave the poems titles, and arranged them thematically. On occasion, some editor would even lop off an unwanted stanza that reopened an interrogation that by the end of the poem should have been closed. Feminist criticism of the 1970s, in turn, would read her, 30s fashion, in terms of cultural context and sexual identity, suppressing the ambiguities of history and gender.

On the issue of difficulty, Dickinson is a slippery poet to deal with, because there are times when she appears infinitely accessible and clear—until she has teased us into a strange space or depth where nothing is its solid self. Two summers ago I was in Uruguay, where I grew up, and I was asked to return to my old high school to give a talk to 13- and 14-year-olds on Dickinson. I decided to evade difficulty altogether, and chose a poem that appeared almost transparent in its theme and its direction:

A narrow Fellow in the Grass
Occasionally rides—
You may have met Him—did you not
His notice sudden is—

The Grass divides as with a Comb—
A spotted shaft is seen—
And then it closes at your feet
And opens further on—

He likes a Boggy Acre
A Floor too cool for Corn—
Yet when a Boy, and Barefoot—
I more than once at Noon
Have passed, I thought, a Whip lash
Unbraiding in the Sun
When stooping to secure it
It wrinkled, and was gone—

Several of Nature's People
I know, and they know me—
I feel for them a transport
Of cordiality—

But never met this Fellow
Attended, or alone
Without a tighter breathing
And Zero at the Bone—

There is fear in this poem, and it is not unreasonable to connect that fear to the slimy and slithering figure of the snake. Yet the child (boy, girl—another whole story here) is curious without being fearful. He attempts to touch it, and the creature propels itself by wrinkling up and shooting forward—and it is gone. The meditation of the poem has nothing to do with fear of snakes. It has to do with the disappearance of an object without a trace of its passage. The grass opens with the passage of the snake, then closes up again, as if that passage had never taken place.

All this takes place "at Noon," a moment of coincidence and perfection, a moment of "identity." Identity is so problematic in Dickinson that even the terms "self," "soul," and "consciousness" seem to be opposed to it rather than synonymous with it. In another poem (1056) Dickinson imagines a moment so perfect that "Consciousness is Noon": self and world, consciousness and its reflection, become one. All otherness disappears at this moment, giving way to an unimaginable oneness. The self is transparent to itself, and transparent in the perpendicular light of the sun.

At Noon, in "A narrow Fellow in the Grass," there is no such coincidence, almost as if these poems were written under the sign of an eclipse. The snake disappears without a trace, the grass springs back as if nothing had ever divided it. And the fear is that the self, too, may leave no trace of itself, that it may be, as Freud suggests, a fiction that we weave about ourselves, a fiction of identity that in Dickinson's poems explodes into alterity. In the lingo of American ego psychology, alterity can be subsumed within identity, just as the unconscious can be rendered transparent and assimilated by the ego. But Dickinson resists such transparence or assimilation. What we are left with in this poem is an absence that nothing can fill, a gap that is constitutive of what Dickinson calls "Soul" and that in this poem she terms "Zero at the Bone." Zero is a "number" that stands for no-number. If you multiply or subtract or add in relation to it, nothing happens. An entity that is not an entity, that is defined only by what is not there, triggers the unreasonable fear at the passage of the snake. At the "heart" or "center" of ourselves, skeleton or soul, stands the Zero, a circumference signifying absence. When in another poem Dickinson says that she "went out upon Circumference / Beyond the Dip of Bell," she is suggesting that she went out into nothing, a nothing that is epitomized by the outer reaches of the universe, but also by the innermost reaches of what we call a "self." In the deepest relationship with ourselves, identity is interrupted by contradiction or alterity, so that to see ourselves is to see that we are not "ourselves," a "self."

To feel "real," we have to be able to leave a mark, to mark our passage through the world, but above all, to mark our passage through ourselves. But if all we are is memories narrated along the lines of desire, what mark or trace can we hope to leave of our passage? What mark or trace can a poem—which is also a "passage"—hope to leave? Dickinson knows this, and her poems function as intervals, interruptions, gaps—moments in consciousness in which consciousness is aware of what is not there, what it cannot comprehend—its "death." Walter Benjamin tells us that we read in order to find out about endings, in the hope that they will teach us about our own end, which we can never experience or appropriate. Dickinson unveils the futility of that hope. At their most powerful, her poems interrupt, breach, wound what we call consciousness or identity or self or the "real Me." Stealthily, like the snake crawling out of trace in the grass, she enacts a disappearance, which is our own.

I would not dream of burdening 13- and 14-year-olds with this meditation. But I did ask them what they might define as frightening, and the discussion moved from monster movies, where gory-looking creatures become visible on screen, to more invisible and more frightening things—things whose effects you can feel, but whose causes you cannot see—like the ramifications of a snake passing through the grass, like the feeling of not being "fully here." Identity, ego, consciousness—these are the hope of presence, reality, self. Dickinson interrupts that presence with her famous dashes, and those dashes become tropes for what cannot be named, for what cannot be understood, comprehended, seen, assimilated into consciousness, wrought into identity. While this may be too abstract even for 18-year-olds, it can be rendered more accessible by invoking, as a first step, cultural artifacts they do know. The photograph album, the souvenir, the collection, as Stewart (1984) has shown us, raise these kinds of issues of appropriation and estrangement. At the most obvious level, Dickinson can be thematized and brought under control. We can say that she is cloistered, in love, out of touch. Or that poems about snakes are really poems about snakes. But if we let her difficulty have its range, we will see why she defines herself as an interval, "the term between." "I found the words for every thought / I ever had—but One—" she says. And that one thought for which there is no name and that renders what is known and named a fragment is what we term death: an absence of consciousness from itself, a fragmented self, a fragmentary text. The dash is not a dash in Dickinson. It is a trope for what cannot be uttered, for what is unnameable and unteachable, but which we need to try to teach again and again.

It may be that this kind of reading of Dickinson, which begins with a deceptive simplicity and proceeds to tease out the difficulties and the alienness, would cure students of reading Dickinson for a long time. But perhaps it also needs to be said again and again that education is in its very nature an elitist proposition. Its purpose is not to translate difficulty into concepts assimilable by culture but, on the contrary, to estrange, to ask what is constitutive of knowledge and the process we call thinking, and to render the culture that surrounds us and that we take for granted problematic. To teach about difficulty is in some sense to work against the grain of educational efficiency, yet there may be no more important task in American higher education. At some point, Dickinson ceases to be translatable into available cultural terms, and that is the area students must be enticed to enter if they are to engage in the difficult work of thought.

But what of poets who are more available, who yield themselves to our understanding without taking us into the circuitous paths of Dickinson? Is level of difficulty going to become the standard for canonicity? Or is difficulty embedded in the critical assumptions we bring to texts? This is the unanswerable question Longinus raises in a different key when he asks whether a poem's power is derived from genius or technique. His answer bypasses (or exceeds) his question: the power of the poem has to do with a moment of figuration in which the reader feels she has created what she has only heard. We may term this moment internalizing, even appropriation, but it is also the other side of estrangement. Dickinson is obviously more "difficult" than Frost, yet this does not mean that Frost cannot be problematized.

When Frost ends his major poem, "Directive," with the injunction to "Drink and be whole again beyond confusion," he is speaking a particularly American dialect. He is suggesting, as formalism did, that difficulty can be transcended, that fragmentation is just a departure from normative wholeness. Frost is known as the simple, straightforward, accessible poet, yet his simplest poems are not so easy to deal with. "The Road Not Taken," for instance, appears to be a poem about choice. Yet choice, with all its humanistic implications of selfhood, authority, mastery over our lives, turns out to be another name for chance. Frost's efforts in the poem are directed toward stating the difference between this road and that, and narrating a sequence of events (I chose this road, and I have ended up here, and I will be telling this same story in the future). He articulates a narrative that comes to some sort of end in a proleptic/retrospective meditation, underwritten by a cause-and-effect etiology. Yet the poem, like the case history of the Wolf Man, doubles back upon itself to tell the opposite story. While he states the differences between one road and another, Frost also tells us that both roads are ultimately the same—trod and worn the same, equally inviting—and his choice, or what he terms his choice, is a random one. "Way leads to way" with frightening randomness, and each step makes the past (the fork, the moment of choice, the possibility of foresight) irretrievable. This is a dark and devious poem, suggesting that the choices we make are chancy choices, and that only belatedly, "ages and ages hence," do we construct a pattern and a direction for our choice. We tell ourselves that our initial choice is "[what] has made all the difference," but choice is the retrospective fiction that we weave about our lives, in an attempt to contain the more dangerous "difference" that undoes our potential for wholeness.

Dickinson confronts us with extreme metaleptic reversals that throw off the possibility of chronology or narrative sequence. But because Frost seems to settle so strongly on such a sequence, the tendency to take him at his word, to not double back, is overwhelming. Frost appears already so thoroughly thematized that he provides us with a surface hard to break. And one might well ask—why should we want to break it? Why not just take it for what it is, for the enjoyment it provides? Why cannot a poem about a choice of two roads be a poem about choices that affect our lives? Because that hard surface functions as "what goes without saying," a given that inhibits thought, and we need to raise the kinds of questions that will get our students "lost" rather than "found." They need to know that moving from "a poem about two roads" to "a poem about choices that affect our lives" is already an interpretation, a trope, and that a reading worthy of its name does not stop there. In this respect, reading involves making a text work against itself, against its own smooth, seamless surface, and perhaps in this light Frost requires a lot more work than Dickinson.

If the work of theory is a problematizing of reading, a teasing out of difficulty, then theory stands in an oppositional relation to the institution. This is not only because institutional pressure is toward method, efficiency, communication, and the rigorous reliability of science, but more importantly because theory ultimately puts the institution itself into question—its role, its organization, its relation to knowledge. For a variety of reasons, the sciences (especially the social sciences) have fit in well with institutional demands and flourished in the academy. It is now the job of the humanities to problematize "method" and engage the classroom and the university in the paths of difficulty.

REFERENCES

Adorno, T. K. (1973). *Negative Dialectics,* trans. E. B. Ashton, New York: Continuum.

Alloula, M. (1986). *The colonial harem.* Minneapolis: University of Minnesota Press.

Aristotle. *Poetics,* trans S. H. Butcher. In H. Adams, ed., *Critical theory since Plato.* New York: Harcourt Brace Jovanovich.

Brooks, P. (1984). *Reading for the plot.* New York: Random House.

Bruns, G. (1989). *Heidegger's estrangements: Language, truth, and poetry in the later writings.* New Haven: Yale University Press.

Culler, J. (1982). *On deconstruction.* Ithaca: Cornell University Press.

———. (1987). "Criticism and its institutions: The American university." In D. Attridge et al, eds., *Poststructuralism and the question of history.* Cambridge: Cambridge University Press.

de Man, P. (1984). *The rhetoric of romanticism.* New York: Columbia University Press.

Derrida, J. (1982). *Margins of philosophy* (A. Bass, Trans.). Chicago: University of Chicago Press.

Godzich, W. (1988). "Emergent literature and the field of comparative literature." In C. Koelb and S. Noakes, eds., *The comparative perspective on literature.* Ithaca: Cornell University Press.

Hartman, G. H. (1987). *The unremarkable Wordsworth.* Minneapolis: University of Minnesota Press.

Heidegger, M. (1977). *Basic writings.* New York: Harper and Row.

Jacobus, M. (1986). *Reading woman.* New York: Columbia University Press.

Johnson, T. H., ed. (1955). *The poems of Emily Dickinson,* 3 vols. Cambridge, MA: The Belknap Press of Harvard University Press.

Lukacher, N. (1986). *Primal scenes.* Ithaca: Cornell University Press.

Miller, N. K., ed. (1986). *The poetics of gender.* New York: Columbia University Press.

Nietzsche, F. W. (1873). "On truth and falsity in their ultramoral sense." In O. Levy, ed. (1964). *The complete works of Friedrich Nietzsche* (vol. 2). New York: Russell and Russell.

Orr, L. (1986). "The revenge of literature: A history of history." *New Literary History,* 18 (1) (Autumn).

Plato. *Theatetus.* B. Jowett (1875). *The dialogues of Plato.* Vol. 4. Oxford: The Clarendon Press.

Spivak, G. C. (1989). "Imperialism and sexual difference." In R. C. Davis and R. Schleifer, eds., *Contemporary literary criticism: Literary and cultural studies* (2nd ed.). New York: Longman.

Stewart, S. (1984). *On longing.* Baltimore: Johns Hopkins University Press.

Vickers, N. J. (1986). "The mistress in the masterpiece." In N. K. Miller, ed., *The poetics of gender.* New York: Columbia University Press.

Warner, W. B. (1986). *Chance and the text of experience.* Ithaca: Cornell University Press.

White, H. (1973). *Metahistory.* Baltimore: Johns Hopkins University Press.

―――. (1978). *Tropics of discourse.* Baltimore: Johns Hopkins University Press.

Young, R. (1981). *Untying the text.* Boston: Routledge and Kegan Paul.

II

Difficulty in Practice and Theory

5.

Kinds of Understanding, Kinds of Difficulties in the Reading of Literature

Gunnar Hansson

Making out the plain sense of an ordinary prose text, and thus following a description or a line of argument, is generally considered to be less difficult than seeing the implied meanings and finding the essential message in a literary text. Although this opinion can certainly be justified, it is still a matter of interest to consider the opposite possibility: when the implied meanings, the unifying tone or the emotional impact as a matter of fact make it easier—for some readers, with some texts—to see and understand the meaning of a literary text. When such cases occur, as they do in both practical teaching and empirical research, they provide insights into the kinds of difficulties that readers meet in literary texts, and into the strategies that readers use when they create and organize meanings.

Another common opinion, often advocated by teachers of literature, is that a reader who maintains that he or she has understood a text but cannot say much about what this understanding is, should not be taken seriously. Meanings that cannot be described and verbalized have not been understood, runs the standard argument. But if we can discern different levels or stages in the processes where readers consecutively produce, structure, analyze, and describe meanings in texts, then forms of understanding other than the fully verbalized ones should perhaps be accepted—particularly so if the readers themselves regard them as rewarding and valuable reading experiences that have a strong personal impact. Discerning such levels or stages in the reading process also implies that we may recognize various kinds of difficulties: for instance, difficulties in organizing meanings that a reader has produced will differ from the difficulties he or she has in verbalizing and communicating these meanings.

In this paper I shall consider these questions, and some others related to them. And I shall do so by viewing them in the light of results from empirical research on the reading process. Such results are often useful material to think with—not because they make thinking more productive, but rather because they help to keep thinking closer to basic facts and processes.

LITERATURE AND ORDINARY PROSE

If some of the Swedish data from the International Association for the Evaluation of Educational Achievement (IEA) in Reading Comprehension and Literature are calculated as percentile values, as they are in Figure 1, some thought-provoking differences between the understanding of literary texts and the understanding of ordinary prose texts are brought out.

These IEA data were collected in 1970 (Purves, 1973; Thorndike, 1973; Hansson, 1975). The degree or level of understanding among 14- and 18-year-old students was registered by a well-verified instrument, using series of multiple-choice questions. In the reading comprehension part of the study the texts were of ordinary prose type: informative, explanatory, or descriptive texts, for instance, of a kind that is regularly found in school books. In the literature part, the texts were short stories written by established authors. They were supposed to be unknown to the students but of a kind that might be studied in a literature course. Only the results for the 18-year-old population are discussed here. Results are shown for four of the three-year lines and for the four-year technical line of the Swedish gymnasium school. These lines are normally chosen by students who want to continue their education on the university level. Results are also shown for some of the two-year gymnasium lines normally leading more directly into various professions in society.

One thing that becomes evident in Figure 1 is that the difference between high- and low-achieving students is much less in literature than in reading comprehension. This is certainly not an expected result: most teachers of mother tongue would readily describe their experiences of students having great difficulties with literary texts but no or few difficulties with ordinary prose texts. To some extent, this difference in the results may be due to the measuring instrument, the potential scale being more compressed in the literature test, for instance. Undoubtedly, however, the difference also depends on more or less divergent processes in the reading and interpretation of the two kinds of texts. Further evidence for such conclusions is provided by a later study (Spenke, 1982). The data for this study were collected in 1976—six years after the IEA data were collected. The same measuring instruments were used, and students from the same lines of the gymnasium school were included in the population of 1976.

Figure 1. Percentile Values, Reading Comprehension and Literature, Swedish Students, 18-years-old, IEA 1970

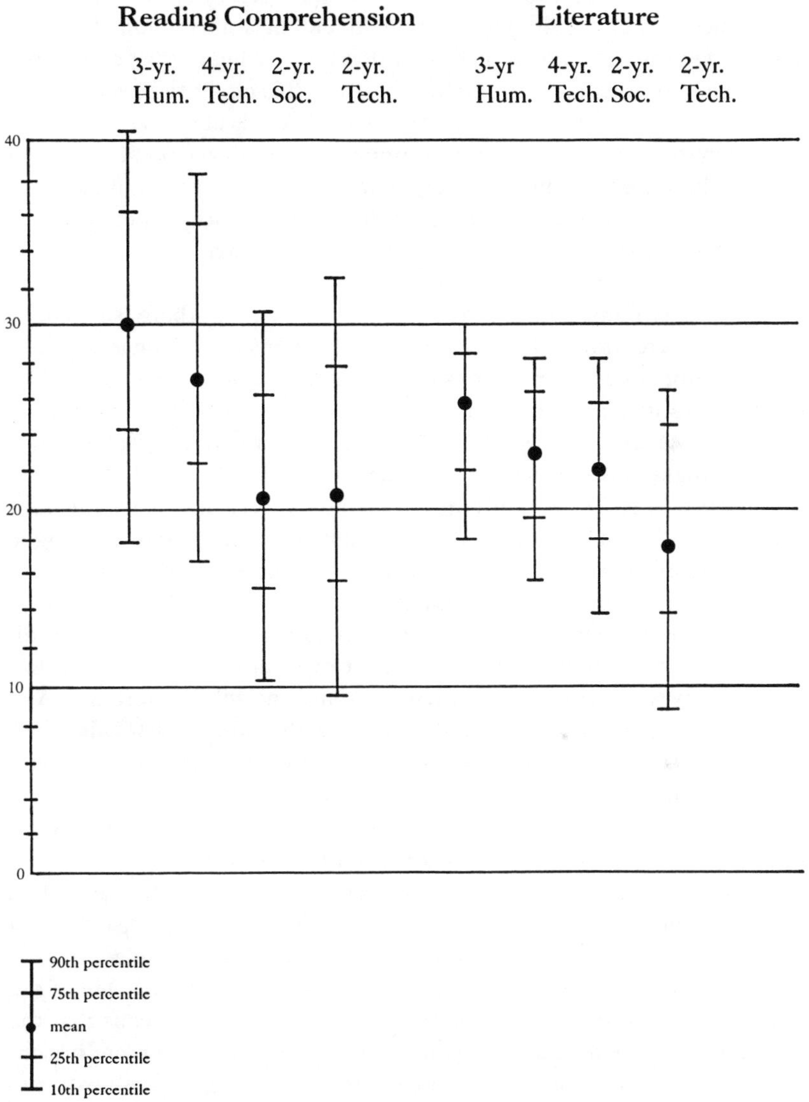

In Figure 2 some of the results from the 1976 investigation have been placed "in front of" the corresponding results from the original IEA study in 1970, in order to facilitate comparisons. Most striking is that the reading comprehension results from 1976 are so much below the corresponding results from 1970. This applies to all percentile levels, but it is particularly so for the weaker students and for students on the two-year lines. On the whole, the difference or distance between high- and low-achieving students has also increased considerably in a short period of only six years. This indicates a severe drop in the general reading ability among Swedish students who are leaving the gymnasium school, either to start a university education or to enter working life. In itself, this ought to be something to observe for teachers of all subjects and on all levels of the Swedish educational system, since the ability to understand ordinary prose texts is a prerequisite for every kind of study, as well as for taking part in all kinds of activities and processes in a modern democratic society. Therefore, the results should also be a reminder for school administrators and politicians who have a responsibility for the Swedish school system.

Another striking thing in Figure 2 is, however, that there is no corresponding severe drop in the literature results. On some gymnasium lines there is a drop, to be sure, but to some extent this drop is out-weighted by improved results on other lines. Furthermore, the drop affects the better part of the students at least as much as the weaker part, and the distance between high- and low-achieving students is rather less in 1976 than it was in 1970. This is certainly not what people in general would have expected, and least of all perhaps what most teachers of mother tongue would have expected. A common line of argument, even among teachers, would most probably be that students who find it difficult and in many cases fail to understand descriptive, explanatory, and other kinds of ordinary prose texts, would most often find it even more difficult to understand literary texts with their implied meanings and subtle overtones. And yet the results demonstrated in Figure 2 clearly indicate that this is not the case—that instead people with less reading experience and training (two-year lines) and lower general reading proficiency (low-achieving students) can find it easier to create, structure, and organize meanings when reading literary texts than when reading ordinary prose texts.

It should be emphasized here that these results, in literature as well as in reading comprehension, were obtained with instruments using a range of multiple-choice questions. The students were then asked to select from or evaluate four preformulated answers to each of the questions. One of the four answers was regarded as the expected answer, which means that the researchers when constructing the instruments regarded it as more reasonable or in some sense better than the other three answers. These expectations were then checked and to some extent modified in pretests, before the main data collection took place. Choosing among such preformulated answers is certainly a different and perhaps also an easier task than when students have to produce their own answers or write protocols with full descriptions and analyses of the meanings of texts they have read. This latter aspect of the meaning-producing process will be discussed further on.

Figure 2. Percentile Values, Reading Comprehension and Literature, Swedish Students, 18-years-old, IEA 1970 and Spenke 1976

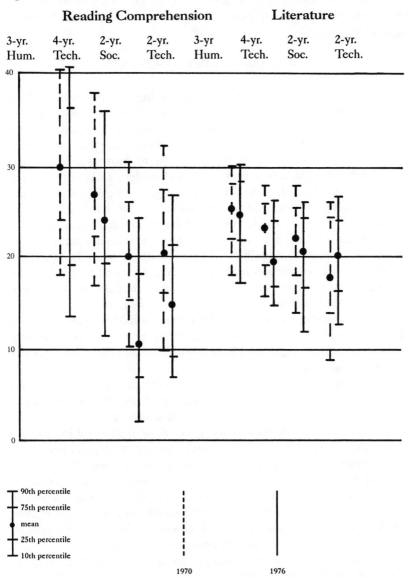

However, if it does occur—as it evidently did in the investigations using the IEA instruments—that literary texts are in some ways easier to understand than ordinary prose texts, then the question whether there are any plausible explanations arises of why this is so. Is there any further empirical evidence available to substantiate such explanations? Would such explanations have any consequences for the way teachers and researchers are looking upon understanding literary texts, or for the way we are looking upon the question of difficulties in people's understanding of literary texts?

IMMEDIATE UNDERSTANDINGS

In research on response to literature using the protocol method, whether in written or oral form, readers often make statements to the effect that the poem or story has made a strong and profound impact, although the reader cannot say very much about what the impact is or what the significant meaning of the text is. In my own research, particularly with some texts or with some groups of readers, I have often found statements like the following: "It makes a great impact on me, and I have a sense that it deals with very essential matters, but I can't explain what it is." "It moves me deeply, and I can follow the meaning of the words line for line, but the total meaning of the text evades me, or I can't find words enough to describe it." The researcher when handling the protocols, as well as teachers in the classroom, often find themselves at a loss as to what to do with these reactions since they do not lend themselves to further analysis, little informative as they are. The researcher may have to put them aside, calling them unclassifiable or miscellaneous, while teachers find their analytic efforts being better rewarded in communications with students who have acquired a more developed descriptive and critical language.

Sometimes, however, and particularly if the research design is such that the readers report on their understanding of the text on two or more occasions in the experimental situation, there will be more information available about what the readers felt, grasped, or understood in their initial readings. Several ways to obtain such consecutive reports have been used, in my own investigations as well as in those carried out by others. Teaching sessions, group discussions, background information about the text or about its author, and textual analyses of different kinds are some examples of means that have been introduced after the initial reading and the writing of the first report. This report has then been followed by a second report, or sometimes by several consecutive reports.

To illustrate this process I shall present in translation from Swedish some protocols from one of my own investigations (Hansson, 1959). (In translation, the protocols appear somewhat more fluent then they do in the original Swedish.) The readers I quote were university students of literature or of psychology, and also 18-year-old students in the gymnasium school. Male and female readers are about equally represented. In order to make statements and references in the quotations from the protocols somewhat more comprehensible, all the illustrations except two are taken from readings of one poem, a condensed and suggestive piece of poetry in the modernistic tradition. It was written by Gunnar Ekelöf, one of the leading Swedish poets, and was first published in 1934. It is called "Autumn Magic" (or Autumn *sejd*, *sejd* being a word for a specific Norse kind of magic, known from old Islandic writings. It was practiced by a man or a woman, sitting on a high stool delivering dark and often threatening messages. It could be used for instance to prophesy the future, to avert disaster, or to inflict damage on other people.) The poem is presented here in a verbatim translation:

Autumn Magic

Be quiet, be silent and wait,
    wait for the wild beast, wait for the foreboding that shall
come,
    wait for the wonder, wait for the destruction that shall come
    when time has got insipid.
It shall soar with stars put out, passing blazing skerries.
It shall come at dawn or at dusk.
Day or night shall not be its time.
When the sun sets in dust and the moon in stone it shall
come
    with stars put out on charred ships...
Then the bloody doors shall be opened for everything
possible.
Then the bloodless doors shall be closed for ever.
The ground shall be filled with unseen steps and the air
with unheard sounds,
    the towns shall fall down on time like strokes of the clock,
    the shells of the ears shall burst like deep in the water
    and time's immeasurable meekness shall be perpetuated
    deep down in dead eyes, in dull lights
    by the wonder that touches upon their houses.
Be quiet, be silent and wait,
    breathless until dawn opens its eye and breathless
    until dusk closes its look.

In some cases the readers indicated already in their first reports that they had a fairly clear idea of their understanding, although they were vague about the meaning in a more limited sense. This is illustrated in the following quotation from a protocol written by a student of psychology:

> The poem creates a feeling of coldness and unpleasantness. One
> is surrounded by darkness and gloominess. Dark colors and
> wide, dark waters appear in one's consciousness.... At the first
> reading, the poem gives an impression of confusion and empti-
> ness. I feel restless. There are symbolic meanings, and I feel like
> having nothing to take hold of, nothing to stick to. My thoughts
> have no foothold. Acoustic and visual images come in rapid suc-
> cession and are just as rapidly stopped. There is agitation in my
> consciousness.

This reader certainly had some understanding of the structuring and
totality of the poem as he read it, although he could not go very far in
describing and analyzing his understanding. In other similar cases the
first report indicates that the reader has tried to find and describe a more
intellectualized meaning, beyond a strongly felt structural unity of other
qualities. The following report from a female university student is one of
many such examples:

> The soft rhythm, the alliterations, the repetitions and the asso-
> nances are combined into a unity which creates a light feeling of
> pleasure.... I have difficulties finding the meaning in it; some-
> how I resist analyzing and taking to pieces (probably because I
> lack training and knowledge). But the feeling it creates, beside
> the experience of its language, is a strange mixture of fear and
> longing. Destruction and miracle are there at the same time.
> The light atmosphere of waiting dominates on the whole.

After the first report this reader was presented with an analysis of the
poem. In the analysis many details of the text were connected with various phenomena of the everyday world (World War II, the Bible), and the
intellectual meaning and structuring of the text were described. The
reader then gratefully accepted the statements in the analysis as the
meaning of the poem as she had understood it in her first reading: "Yes,
now the poem has got its so-called meaning, which I was looking for previously." Her statement, and similar statements by other readers in the
same situation, should be taken to indicate that there is a level of understanding that precedes or perhaps is below or beside that kind of intellectual understanding that can be fully described in words and thus communicated to others. This is perhaps even more clearly demonstrated in such
cases where the readers, having the same kind of clearly felt or *seen* but to
some extent unformulated initial experience, do not accept the interpretation which is presented to them later on. Such cases are also quite common. The following quotation, also from a female university student, is
one example from the same investigation and relating to the same poem:

Wonderful, suggestive rhythm, which is strengthened by the alliterations. The rhythm in itself transmits an atmosphere of trembling expectation. The poem makes a very strong impression through its rapid heightening to a crescendo... which then falls to quiet peace. I think it symbolizes every great, purifying, revolutionary event, and also the greatness of what is small, seemingly unimportant, and commonplace. What is important is less what the words mean than their tone together.... Purging and revival. Death or birth. Life itself, the mystery of growth. You can see biblical influences, both in the choice of words and in the poem's mixture of feelings of disaster and blissful expectation. But I think that what is essential in the poem, what it expresses, is an awe-inspiring exultation over the greatness of life. The mixture of words from the most different areas gives rise to long files of associations and is the reason why I cannot find in the poem more—or less—than a general, all-embracing feeling like the one I have tried to describe. That is probably why I find the poem so beautiful, apart from the rhythm and the fine harmony of the words.

An all-embracing feeling, the perceived rhythm of the poem as the reading proceeds, the tone of the words together more than their meaning, are basic qualities of this first reading of the text. And yet, when this particular reader was presented with an analysis of the poem, an analysis in which the meaning of the poem was discussed in more discursive terms than the reader had done, it turned out that she had a clear and distinct view of what the poem did mean and what it did not. She started to argue about the descriptions and interpretations presented in the analysis and put forward a number of reservations and qualifications: the basic feeling is not fearful waiting but fearful expectation, autumn is not only a time for corruption but also for purification, it is followed by winter with rest and peace before a new spring, and so forth.

Readings and interpretations like the ones I have illustrated here are often looked down upon or even dismissed by teachers, critics, and literary theorists: they are said to be too vague, too emotional, too little concerned with the meaning of the text, too little related to the actual wording and structuring of the text. Such attitudes are questionable, particularly from a researcher's point of view, but also in many teaching situations. There are, as is already indicated by the few examples I have given, many such readings that are neither vague nor particularly emotional. On the contrary, they are often quite advanced understandings of the poems, although they have been less intellectualized and less put into the kind of discursive terms and analytical phrases that teachers and critics have been taught to use. The lack of this analytic-discursive dimension in a report or protocol does not necessarily imply vagueness in the understanding or excessively emotional qualities in the reading. The often very strong expressions of personal involvement and appreciation, which are quite common ingredients in these reports, may just as well be taken to indicate preciseness in the understanding. At least in my own experience of empirical research, any collection of reports from a group of readers—young or old, with high or low education—will contain much evidence of such readings with strong personal involvement, but less intellectual analysis and description.

One feature of these readings is that the understanding of the text has been reached through a synthetic, immediate, and seemingly almost effortless grasp of the total impact of the words. This approach to the text often means listening to the words, images, and associations, and finding in them a total configuration, which is then described as the meaning, the impact, the personal and often very valuable experience of the text. In many cases such readings bring the literary experience quite close to the experience of a piece of music, and it is not unusual for readers to use descriptive words with explicit or implicit references to music:

> Cheerfully inviting, eager and fussy, mildly singing, the author's exclamations are crowding together. . . . Somewhat abruptly comes this philosophical thought after all the practical cares, comes like the last tunes of a small melody softly dying away.

> First I was deeply moved by the suggestive, silently intensive opening. . . . Then the mood suddenly reversed, I have an impression of piercingly strong and clear movements. . . . Finally comes—like repetition and reminding of the meek mood in the first part—the final line, which rounds off the poem like the resting final chord on the keynote in a piece of music.

In other cases the synthetic experience is of a more dramatic kind, described by the readers themselves as movements or configurations in their minds, sometimes light and pleasing, sometimes strong and even threatening, as is illustrated in these reports from two 18-year-old students:

> It makes me vibrate deep down—in the beginning lightly, then more strongly. The climax is reached with "the ground shall be filled with. . . ." Then the mood passes over into the mysterious and breathless. . . . The conflicting elements create a mysterious feeling, difficult to describe.

> To me it was as if something that had been forgotten for a long time, for thousands of years, rose and responded within me. My

normal, coldly calculating being stood beside, powerless against this primeval gray. . . . Everything, absolutely everything, is revoked. I think it is something fantastic, my mind reels, I want to scream but cannot, only wait, wait. But after this stormy climax, a few soft final chords follow.

In other cases the unifying element may be a different kind of movement, the reader having an impression of being moved from one scene to another during the process of reading, and ending up in a coherent experience felt to be very valuable, loaded with meaning. Such is the case in the following report, which relates to a poem describing a light summer night with streaks of mist moving to and fro:

> This part creates a lasting impression of rapid changes in the scene. . . . I am now an onlooker. I am not "taking part" in the action any more. . . . The scene is suddenly swept clean . . . now all is visible again . . . now again I am brought in among the misty figures. . . . It is as if everything is dissolved into nothing, or into a light *wind*, and I have a strong impression of infinity, and of my own smallness.

Such understandings are vague only in the sense that they do not go very far in analytic descriptions of the detailed meanings and the structuring of such meanings. In another sense, however, they need not be vague at all, since readers often have very clear ideas of both the central import and the structuring of their reading:

> The composition of the poem is simple and logical. The first and last lines create a frame and provide the basic atmosphere of the vision of destruction, which forms the center and climax of the poem. . . . The poem creates in me as reader the same feeling as when I am watching a slowly rising wave; it rises higher and higher and then collapses, and then slowly withdraws again.

Readings of this kind are often saturated with personal feelings and values, which, as the preceding examples have shown, stand out very clearly in the minds of the readers themselves, both as to their essential meaning and as to their form and structure. Perhaps as a result of previous teaching or other experiences of the same kind, many readers are also eager to defend their own subtle understanding and to protect it from outside influence, as is illustrated in the following report, written by an 18-year-old girl:

> The destruction is described vaguely, but it is strongly moving. I do not know what constitutes it, perhaps a war or the Day of Judgment. But, I don't care if nobody tells me about this. The

mood of the poem is so moving and harrowing and elusive, it perhaps would be demolished if it was analyzed. The poem is so unspeakably beautiful in its choice of words and expressions and seems so balanced and clear, despite the fact that I don't understand everything in it. Alliterations, repetitions of words and other artistic devices make a strong impression on me.... The poem does not consist of word combinations without sense; I perceive the coherence so strongly, although it is elusive.

It is easy to imagine that synthetic understandings of this kind sometimes touch upon deeply personal layers of experience, which are not confined to what is regarded as aesthetically pleasing or even bearable. The insights that are beginning to take shape in the reading, or the configuration of what is moving around in the reader's mind during the reading process, may be disturbing or even threatening. Such insights, more or less clearly apprehended, are also a kind of understanding, however—an understanding that the reader may try to avoid, prevent, get away from or simply hide by choosing divergent lines to rationalize an interpretation.

Many or most such threatening understandings probably pass unnoticed, both by the teacher and by the researcher. More conspicuous cases will be noticed, however. In my own experience from several investigations there have been some cases that clearly illustrate this kind of reactions among readers. I shall give just one example, provided by a young man studying psychology at the university. The poetry reading session was included as part of the regular psychology course, where it was intended to provide insights into problems in giving introspective reports. Thus, the students were expected to finish the task, and ample time was allowed. The student was disturbed after his first glancing through the text:

> What the hell is the poet trying to frighten us with! This test person's *personality* reacts most strongly and emotionally against this. A parallel with my childhood's horror dreams of the world's destruction is immediate. (Some time at the age of eight or nine I came across a religious brochure from some sect. On the cover of it there was a picture of the world's destruction. This occupied my thoughts very much up to the age of about sixteen, when a kind of scientific relativism helped me against this horror....) But why choose such atrocities as this one! Such a poem (hell, I don't want to call such a thing poetry), surely it would suffice with less mentally unhealthy pieces than this one.... This test person was so utterly frustrated after the first perusal of the produce that he didn't want to look at it any more. Every-

thing offers resistance. . . . But now I am looking at the paper again, and I *cannot* go on reading it.

On some level this man certainly had reached an understanding of the poem, an understanding that could not be very detailed or intellectually analyzed, but that was clear enough for him to realize that he had better stay away from further reading and further analysis. He also used all kinds of maneuvers to get away from the assigned task—some of them are visible in the quotation, others are not. The person administering the session was for instance abused several times, since he was said to be the cause of the reader's unpleasant situation.

SYNTHETIC AND ANALYTIC READINGS

One common feature with the kind of readings and understandings I have illustrated here is that they are formed quite *early* in the reading process. Often readers report that they had a clear idea of the significant meaning, or that they strongly felt the essential import of the poem at the very first reading. Such understandings are rarely reported after much probing or hard thinking with repeated readings—most often they are there quickly and easily, or not at all.

Another common feature is that readers have reached their understanding by a synthetic approach to the texts: not by some kind of analytic effort, looking at the meaning of isolated words, images, or symbols, or at formal elements, structural arrangements, and such things, but by grasping a total configuration, a unifying tone or an expressive movement. Details are always less important than the totality and unity of the experience. Seemingly the unity of the experience has been there almost effortlessly, as an immediate product of the mind following the words and lines of the poem, seeing the connections between them and feeling them organized into a unity expressing essential truths.

A third feature is that most of these readers, when they have arrived at or created such experiences, are quite happy with their interpretation and understanding of the poems. Most of them openly declare that they have no wish to be more specific about the meaning of the poem, no need to analyze it further into details or to find out about possible references to various things and phenomena of the outer world. In their reading the references of the poems are to inner realities, dimensions, and qualities, and to personal values. Some of them do accept suggestions or statements about references to outward realities, about more intellectualized meanings, or about structural configurations in these meanings. But they seldom need them, and few find them helpful in a deeper sense of the word. Others decline such suggestions, or even object to them, because they find them disturbing or upsetting to the subtle balance in their own reading.

Processes and qualities of the kinds I have illustrated are dominant in many readings and understandings. Naturally, they vary with different kinds of poems—some inviting them, others hardly allowing them. And above all, they vary with the readers: some readers seem to prefer such understandings as often as the texts allow them, while other readers seldom or never are content with anything less than a detailed and complete analytic understanding. It is very likely, however, that elements of the kind I have discussed are to some extent present in many or most readings of texts generally regarded as literary texts. Elements of this kind may even be among the basic ingredients in the much discussed *literariness* of such texts. Even if many readers favor more analytic approaches to the texts and want to reach understandings that can be described in discursive and analytic terms, their readings may be permeated, supported, and structured by what is often—but not always very adequately—called emotional qualities.

The presence and the structuring power of such qualities may also be an essential part in the explanation of the differences in the understanding of literary and ordinary prose texts, which were demonstrated in the first part of this paper. The drop in the IEA results from 1970 to 1976 (Figure 2) was much less conspicuous in literature than in reading comprehension, and it was quite evident that students with low reading ability had considerably less difficulties in understanding literary texts than ordinary prose texts. Undoubtedly at least part of the explanation is that literary texts—or rather students reading texts regarded as literary—already in the initial stages of the reading process produce meaning qualities and structural configurations strong enough to build up and hold together a unified and *total* experience of the kind I have illustrated in the preceding pages. They are also strong and *engaging* enough to help weak readers to fill out gaps and overcome other kinds of difficulties in their creation of meaning when reading the texts.

In the reading of ordinary prose texts, such gaps and difficulties might make it impossible to follow the logical argument, to see the assumptions leading up to the final conclusion, or to perceive the connection between different parts of the text. In this way literary texts are often more effective from a communication point of view, since they use—in the sense that they invite readers to use—simpler but stronger means of communication than ordinary prose texts do. In ordinary prose texts the exact meaning of a few key words or the correct analysis of a complicated sentence structure is often crucial for a full understanding of a description or an argument.

CREATING MEANINGS, AND DESCRIBING THEM

The meanings of a literary text are not there on the printed page to be discovered and recognized by readers. Every single meaning and every other quality present in the understanding of a literary text is *created* by the individual reader, taken out of his or her mind and combined with many other qualities in the reading process. Naturally, readers will have different resources in this respect: they have different linguistic backgrounds, they have different life experiences, and, depending among other things on how much exposure to literature they have had and how much training in reading literature they have had, they have different abilities to use the printed words to evoke the linguistic and experiential assets that they actually have in their minds.

The meanings and other qualities that have been evoked in the primary reading process must be organized and structured into larger meaning units. The text is there to guide and give reference points, but the reader is still the active partner: he or she has to be the organizer, to see the connections between different parts, and to accept or reject the many possibilities occurring in his or her mind. Again, individual differences as well as group differences, depending on background, basic resources, and training, will be of vital importance for the creation of structure and coherence in what has been evoked in the reading process. Although the text provides many signals and clues also in this respect, the reader's knowledge of what can and cannot be expected from a poetic or literary text, of strategies that can be used to organize data in one's mind, or of hypotheses to be tested in relation to the text as well as to the reader's life experience, is at least as important.

When a satisfactory and durable organization of the reading experience has been achieved, the next step for readers is to try to make themselves conscious of what the organization is that they have created in their mind: what the impact of it is, why it has moved them so deeply or left them indifferent, what in their previous life experience it is related to, what words would be adequate to describe it or at least point out its contours, and so forth. This is the stage where a new linguistic process is started, a process that goes in the opposite direction, partly parallel with but also growing out of the process in which the words printed on the page get their meanings. Now the reader is searching for and trying out first concepts and then words, descriptive phrases, images, metaphors, and symbols felt to be adequate in relation to what the reader has seen, felt, or grasped in his or her mind while reading the text. This searching for concepts and trying out words and phrases will probably remain incomplete and tentative in many cases, but that does not necessarily mean that what was seen, felt, or grasped by the reader was also incomplete or vague. The illustrations that I have quoted on the previous pages should be evidence enough of this.

Not always but quite often readers of literature want to communicate their understandings and interpretations to others, either orally or in writing. Sometimes they are requested to do so, as they are in the classroom or when they are test subjects in empirical research. This is the stage in which the reversed linguistic process is being fully developed: virtually at a distance readers are then looking back upon their reading, upon the meanings they have created and upon the structuring they have given them. The conscious aim is to try to find descriptive and analytic words that will make it possible for others to understand what they as readers have understood. In its more developed forms—as in essays and formal analyses printed in books and journals—this is a highly complex form of communication, using an acquired specialist language, partly a metalanguage, which only a selected group of people can master. In its less developed forms—as in informal talking or weekly papers in schools—it is a means for training the capacity to discern more and finer qualities and dimensions in one's own readings and to communicate them to others.

The four stages I have mentioned here should not be thought of as isolated stages, one strictly following the other in the reading process. Undoubtedly they roughly cover a temporal sequence in what readers are doing when they create meanings in literary texts. More important, however, is that they are stages in a continuous process in which they are more or less overlapping each other, the mind zigzagging between them rather than moving in a straight line from one to the other. Tentative verbalizations, for instance, will certainly occur in the beginning of the reading process, and structuring or restructuring will continue into the verbalization stage, sometimes even as an effect of the efforts to find adequate descriptive words.

However, if the implications of these four stages are not carried too far, they may be used as a kind of frame for the observations illustrated in this paper. *Understanding* a literary work is not only occurring in the stages where descriptive or analytic words and phrases are produced, and it is not limited to what can be communicated by such words and phrases. Understanding also occurs earlier in the reading process, when the words on the page are given meanings, which are structured and organized into larger meaning units, the essence or import of which is grasped and often deeply valued by the reader. Understandings of the latter kind do not occur with every reader or with every type of text, but they do occur often enough to be of great interest for teachers and researchers alike.

Teachers who are interested not only in what their students can verbalize but also in what they have actually understood while reading a piece of literature, will find it rewarding to try to find out what has taken place in the minds of the students while they were reading. There are several worthwhile tasks for knowledgeable and cautious teachers in the earlier stages of the reading process: helping students create more meanings, helping them structure these meanings, assisting them in making and testing *hypotheses* for structuring and interpreting created meanings, enlarging their store of strategies and verbal tools for interpretation and evaluation, systematically developing the descriptive, interpretive, analytic, and evaluative language that the students have not yet acquired, and so forth.

The natural curiosity of response researchers will invite them to try to find out about and explain mechanisms and functions in all stages of the reading process. The nature of an understanding that is clearly grasped and deeply felt and yet incompletely covered by descriptive words stands out as rather a challenge. How and under what circumstances such understandings are created, and how they can be registered and analyzed, are attached challenges.

My own interest in these aspects of the reading process grew out of an occupation with some problems of interpretation in literature. When literary critics write in their essays and analyses for instance that while there is a strong tragic mood in the first part of the poem, there is a streak of joy coming up in the middle part, or that gloominess in the first stanza and delight in the second are mixed in the third, it is evident that they are not referring to what occurred in the mind of the author of the poem. (Besides having been out of fashion for some time, critical statements with such references would amount to committing the *intentional fallacy*.) Most critics would claim that they are writing about the *text* and that they are referring to meanings "in" the text. In reality they are certainly referring to their own reading of the text, or at least to somebody's reading. (Here some critics would protest vehemently, saying that this would amount to committing the *affective fallacy;* which would not bother the response researcher, however, since he or she knows better.)

Having arrived at this position, it is easy for a response researcher to ask if there are possibilities to find out whether meanings, qualities, or structural configurations that critics have found in particular poems (i.e., in their readings of these poems) could also be found in the readings of different groups of people. In my own thinking the use of verbal scales, similar to those worked out by Charles Osgood and his colleagues (Osgood, 1957), seemed to be a promising possibility. The standard set of scales, often called the semantic differential, would not be the best alternative, however, for the simple reason that this was a standardized set, explicitly intended to register *general* dimensions in people's use of language. In the case of literature, and particularly of course in the case of poetry, *particular* dimensions would be of much greater interest. Thus, scales directly derived from dimensions used by the critics in their interpretations and analyses seemed to be more promising. Put in another way, statements made by the critics would be used as *hypotheses* concerning meanings in other people's readings.

This was done in a first study (Hansson, 1964), using a Swedish poem divided into a number of sections, each being a complete meaning—carrying unit (apart, of course, from their relations to the other sections). A series of twenty-five scales was constructed, some of them taken from the original Osgood set, but most of them derived from statements made by critics. The scales were of the original bipolar, seven-point type, with a *neutral* point in the middle. Three groups of readers, widely different in respect to reading experience, training in literature, and level of formal education, were asked to judge each successive sector of the poem on the whole series of scales.

The three groups of readers did not find it difficult to use the scales, and the results demonstrated without doubt that the scales helped the readers to observe and also judge subtle meaning dimensions, which many of them, particularly in the groups with least training in reading, could hardly have described or discussed in written protocols. Even more surprising, however, was that the three groups of readers, in spite of the great differences in education and reading experience, made almost the same observations and judgments on the scales. This indicates that the readers in all three groups had been able to create and organize understandings of the poem, in which they could discern many of the often quite subtle meanings that the critics had discussed in their analyses. As can be seen in Figure 3, the profiles derived from the means of the judgments made by the members of the three groups, follow each other very closely. The only exceptions were a few scales registering formal qualities (like simple–complex). These scales are not applicable directly to linguistic qualities, but rather to configurations or functions of such qualities, which may make them more dependent on training to be observed.

In a later series of studies (Hansson, 1974) a scale instrument was used in combination with written protocols. Four different poems were studied, and the scales had been modified: instead of bipolar seven-point scales a unipolar type with seven points and a box for "not relevant" or "outside the scale" was used. In this case the scales were derived from "hypotheses" that in their turn were derived from statements by teachers, who had been asked to describe their experiences from using the four poems in their teaching. The readers were students from three different levels of the educational system: the compulsory school (age 16), the gymnasium (age 18), and the university (age 20–25), studying literature.

Figure 3. Means for Three Groups of Readers on the Scale
TRAGIC – HAPPY

TRAGIC – HAPPY

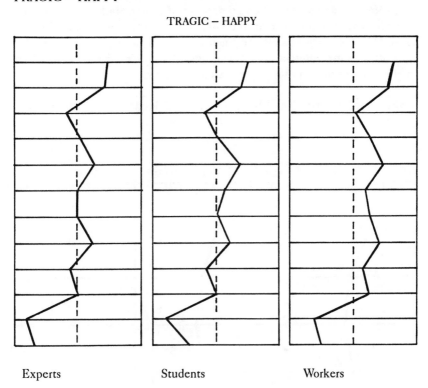

Experts   Students   Workers

Again, the same remarkable correspondence in the scale profiles for the three groups of readers came out in the results of the studies (Figure 4). And again this indicates that in spite of wide differences in age, formal education, and reading experience, the three groups of readers had very similar ability to create meanings in the initial stages of the reading process, and also to organize and observe these meanings when using the scales. When later on they were asked to describe and interpret the poems in written protocols, the similarities were not at all the same, however. The differences between the three groups were great and of kinds that are well known from other studies using written protocols. The younger students with the least training in the reading and analysis of literature often wrote just one or two sentences, which provided incomplete information about their understanding, while older students with more training could produce small essays with detailed descriptions and coherent interpretations. The older students had learned how to use descriptive and often quite expressive language to communicate their understanding, but the younger students seemed to fumble around with insufficient words, although their brief comments sometimes indicated that they had actually reached some kind of understanding. In comparison with the scaled responses the written protocols easily led to the conclusion that such protocols are insufficient and perhaps also unreliable indicators of meaning and understandings that readers have been able to create and observe in the primary reading process.

Figure 4. Means for Three Groups of Readers on the Scale CALM

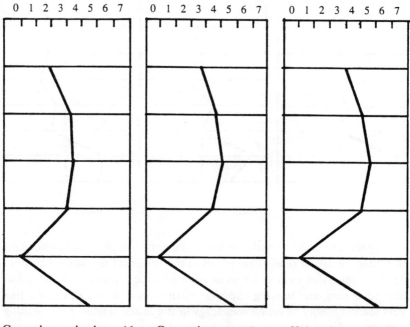

Compulsory school, age 16   Gymnasium, age 18   University, age 20–25

Verbal scales are probably just one of several methods that should be tried in the efforts to reach such early understandings, which to some extent—or sometimes surely to a large extent—remain unformulated, and which, therefore, also remain unrecognized. Other promising methods may already be at hand, and others may be invented by resourceful persons. Readers answering carefully directed questions with brief intervals during the first readings of texts may be one example. Readers indicating when a clear understanding of the text or a particular part of it has been reached, followed by an interview about what the understanding is like, may be another example. Various projective methods, drawing pictures that *describe* the understanding, or even registering bodily reactions while persons are reading or listening to a text, might be worth trying.

KINDS OF UNDERSTANDING, KINDS OF DIFFICULTIES

The illustrations I have given here should have made it clear that synthetic and incompletely verbalized understandings run the risk of being overlooked, in teaching as well as in research. Teachers may never discover them in the classroom, for they are listening for other categories of understanding, and researchers may just put them aside, for they do not match their prearranged criteria for classification. Both teachers and researchers may concentrate on the more fully verbalized understandings, particularly if both are dressed in the kind of fluent critical language and full-fledged analytical terms, that they recognize as their own language.

This is an acquired language, however, and much effort is being devoted in universities and higher levels of schools to mediate it to members of new generations. Not all such members are living under conditions that allow them to acquire this language, and not all find it necessary to do so even if they could. And yet many are continuously reading literature and finding great pleasure in doing so. It is more than likely that they go on doing it because they are understanding what they are reading, although they are more or less lacking the discursive language to describe their understandings. Once the full range of meaning-creating activities has been seen clearly and demonstrated, it will probably be hard to maintain that a description in discursive and analytic language is necessary for understanding to have occurred in the mind of a reader of literature.

Clearly, what should be called understanding in the reading of literature may take place at different stages or levels of the reading process. Fully verbalized descriptions, analyses, and evaluations are one way of obtaining information about these understandings. Primarily, however, they are reports from the final stage of the reading process, and although the kind of understanding that has occurred in the earlier stages may be revealed in such reports, this will in most cases happen indirectly and perhaps incidentally. Other means, like verbal scales, multiple-choice instruments, or directed questions, may be better and more direct ways for the researcher to reveal other levels or depths of understanding. In teaching situations, when there are no written reports, awareness of the different stages of the reading process, a sensitive ear, and an open mind will help teachers to discover more and perhaps deeper understandings than those produced by the most eloquent students in the classroom.

The results I have used as illustrations indicate that difficulties in reading literature may be of several kinds, depending on the stage of the reading process in which they manifest themselves. Generally, the results indicate that many difficulties should be located in the ability of readers to formulate a response that matches the expectations and the criteria of teachers and researchers, rather than in the ability of the readers to create and organize meanings into coherent structures. In such cases the difficulties are not primarily in the reading process but in the process of resymbolization, that is, in the process where what has been understood in a person's reading of a text has to be dressed in new concepts and new words. And, it might be added, preferably what has been understood should be dressed in words and concepts which are in accord with the norms of people who represent the society of the literarily educated.

The results also indicate, however, that there are other kinds of difficulties for the researcher to study and for the teacher to help the students overcome than those that can be observed in a verbalized response. Some readers will have difficulties already in the initial stage of the reading process, when they use the text to produce a wealth of meanings. Particularly with condensed and complicated texts, many of these meanings will be discarded later on or be kept floating in the background. Both the capacity to produce enough meanings and to choose among those that have been produced will vary, depending on many circumstances: the individual's experience with the use of language and with various branches of reality, for instance. It is certainly a capacity that can be trained and developed, both generally and in its more specific applications in the reading of literature.

Other readers, although they may be quite good at producing meanings, will have difficulties in their efforts to organize these meanings into larger units. These units have to be congruent not only with the text and the many signals that can be found there, but also with the individual reader's life experience. The structuring of such units is a highly complicated task, particularly for less experienced readers. Knowledge of norms and conventions that are practiced in the world of literature is one of several prerequisites for their efforts to be successful.

Still other readers will have difficulties in finding paths from the structures they have organized, or from the insights they have gained through these structures, to the verbal resources that they have to use in order to clarify in discursive language—to themselves or to others—what they have seen or felt in their reading. This is where the more coherent verbalization of the understanding of the literary text is being started, and for most readers it is a long way to go and there are many difficult steps to practice from the initial stage of the reading process.

REFERENCES

Hansson, G. (1959). *Dikten och läsaren* [Poetry and the reader (1st ed.)]. Stockholm: Prisma.

————. (1964). *Dikt i profil* [Poetry in profile]. Göteborg: Akademiförlaget-Gumperts.

————. (1970). *Dikten och läsaren* [Poetry and the reader (2nd ed.)]. Stockholm: Prisma.

————. (1974). *Litteraturläsning i gymnasiet* [Reading literature in the gymnasium]. Stockholm: Utbildningsförlaget.

————. (1975). *Läsning och litteratur* [Reading and literature]. Stockholm: Almqvist and Wiksell International.

Osgood, C. E., Suci, G. J. and Tannenbaum, P. H. (1957). *The measurement of meaning.* Urbana: University of Illinois Press.

Purves, A. C. (1973). *Literature education in ten countries.* Stockholm: Almqvist and Wiksell.

Spenke, C. (1982). *Läsa, lära, förstå* [Read, learn, understand]. Lund: Gleerup.

Thorndike, R. L. (1973). *Reading comprehension education in fifteen countries.* Stockholm: Almqvist and Wiksell.

6.

Questions of Difficulty in Literary Reading

Susan Hynds

Teacher questioning techniques have long been heralded as a vehicle for reducing the difficulty of literary interpretation, as a means of testing how students grapple with that difficulty, and as a way of increasing students' interpretive skills by leading them through progressively "higher" levels of thinking. Unfortunately, the ways in which teachers have traditionally used questioning as a means of teaching, testing, and skill-building have often promoted the very interpretive difficulty that these techniques were intended to mitigate. More than this, teachers, through their questioning techniques, have often encouraged students to look for easy answers rather than to grapple with the essential complexity and incompleteness of literary texts.

Over the past several years, the reading of literature has been increasingly viewed as a social interpretive process. As poststructuralist theories of literary criticism and socio-cognitive views of discourse development have gained prominence, conceptions of the reading process have changed from a largely cognitive phenomenon of print decoding to a socially situated process of understanding and appropriating a variety of discourse and text conventions.

In a social view of reading (Hynds, in press), readers always operate from particular interpretive contexts. Thus, "difficulty" is not a feature of particular texts, but the result of the similarity or disparity between dimensions of the text and the socially embedded and motivated interpretive processes of particular readers.

In literature classrooms on the secondary level and beyond, students must learn to "read" not only particular literary texts, but the codes, conventions, and interpretive norms of a particular teacher's classroom. Thus, one *difficulty* of school reading is that students must often "reinterpret" their immediate perceptions of literary texts, in order to balance or bring their views into conformity with the views of the teacher and the classroom literary community.

The comments of Ken (names are fictitious), a 12th-grade student, reveal the powerful influence of teachers' questions on his reading and interpretive process:

> K: We'd have these packets and, you know, you'd read a chapter and you'd have questions . . . that you'd answer from the chapter. . . . I remember getting a lot of packets, you know?

> I: How did you feel about those packets?

> K: Uhm, sometimes I thought, you know, I like reading and enjoying the reading, and sometimes the questions that they ask. . . . I thought I read it well and took my time, you know, I couldn't remember, I couldn't get the answer. You'd have to go back and look. . . .

> I: When you're going to read something for classes as opposed to when you just read something because you want to read it, do you read it differently?

> K: A lot of times I'll like, if I get questions that I know I have to answer, I'll look at the questions first and then when I read I'll maybe make a mark or something, you know, . . . cause it's annoying when you have to go back and search through and you know that you remember where it was but you have to search back, but . . . if it's for pleasure I just read carefree. . . . I just read, you know, at whatever pace I want and just enjoy it. I don't really concentrate too much. [Hynds, 1989]

Perhaps the most disturbing aspect of this conversation is that Ken seems to put his interpretive capacities to use, not in exploring the hidden meaning of the literary text, but in interpreting the teacher's not-so-hidden agenda. He has learned, for instance, that reading for school means reading toward a predetermined conclusion. His classroom reading reflects a guessing game in which the teacher's questions guide him toward simple solutions and away from the complex problems of literary interpretation and response.

STUDENTS' PERCEPTIONS OF TEACHER QUESTIONING

The comments of many students reveal how often teacher questions accentuate the difficulty of literary reading, rather than equipping students to deal with it. First, in tending to *simplify* the interpretive process to a quest for "one right answer," teachers' questions often serve to set up a reading stance that turns students away from issues of interpretive complexity. This reductionistic perspective leaves young readers ill-equipped to deal with the interpretive gaps (Iser, 1980) that distinguish literary texts from other kinds of texts. In the previous excerpt, for instance, Ken talks about going back to look through the text and remembering places in order to "get the answer" he is searching for.

In addition, teachers' questions often reveal contradictory expectations about how to succeed in the classroom interpretive community. Teachers may tell students to explore their own unique interpretations, yet send powerful messages through their questions on tests and in class discussions that undermine and undervalue student opinions and hunches. As Jay, a high school senior, muses:

> I don't know. It's supposed to be your language and you're supposed to be able to do it perfectly and English teachers are often like really picky, and everything has to be exactly right. . . . I don't know, for a native language, it comes off like, *hard* . . . especially when it's not like "basic" English. Like when you're reading Shakespeare, poetry—I mean, that's when it's usually the hardest for me.

Thus, in promoting the idea that interpretations must be "exactly right," teachers tend to disempower students in dealing with interpretive difficulty on their own. As they read the underlying messages behind teachers' questions, students often adopt a teacher-dependent, submissive role—a position that holds them back from creating or exploring an innovative or fresh interpretation. Ken's searching back and remembering "where it [the answer] was" in the text is an indication that he views literature as a *container* for *correct meaning*, rather than a fertile ground for exploration and interpretation.

In addition, many approaches to classroom questioning emanate from a cognitivist "reading comprehension" perspective, where students are supposedly led, through increasingly "higher level" questions, toward increasingly complex levels of thought and interpretation (Herber, 1967; Manzo, 1970; Raphael and Pearson, 1982; Stauffer, 1959, 1969). While useful for describing nonliterary reading, such approaches focus almost exclusively on literal or interpretive comprehension, rather than more affective personal responses. Furthermore, it is somewhat simplistic to associate "higher level" questions with higher level thought, and "lower level" questions with purely literal thought (Langer, 1985; 1989).

It is not surprising, for instance, that in reading for pleasure, Ken "reads at his own pace," is "carefree," and just "enjoys it." In Ken's case, his teachers' "prereading" questions often preclude the engagement and exploratory attitude that might have actually invited him to grapple with the difficulty of literary reading. In fact, in an earlier interview, Ken had observed:

> I think that if you're reading a novel ... [teachers] have to know
> if you've read it and stuff like that, you know, they have to ask
> some questions, but ... [they should] ask maybe general ideas of
> the chapter instead of specifics, you know, like ... "describe what
> the character went through" ... something where you'd have to
> think, but you wouldn't have to go searching for the exact quote
> ... which would still, I think, accomplish the same thing,
> because you're actually thinking about what happened and dis-
> cussing it. More interpretive questions than "What happened
> here?" I think. [Hynds, 1989]

Teacher questions from a reading comprehension perspective often
ignore the "literariness" of literary texts, narrowing, rather than broadening, response, and privileging answer-hunting, rather than aesthetic
involvement in the reading act. Ken's strategies of looking at the teacher's questions first and marking the text are appropriate, perhaps, for
studying a history or science text, but entirely inappropriate for reading a
literary work.

Thus, the "difficulty" of literary reading in the classroom goes far
beyond the difficulty of understanding and interpreting texts. Students
must learn to become comfortable with complexity and ambiguity in the
presence of powerful teacher messages that reward simple solutions and
"best" interpretations. They must learn to be independent readers in a
classroom culture that encourages intellectual dependency and adher-
ence to interpretive norms. They must preserve their personal affective
responses in a climate that focuses largely on literal or inferential meaning-making. And finally, they must recognize the "literariness" of literature in an environment where tests and skill-building activities predomi-
nate. It is time for a reconceptualization of what we mean by
"understanding" literary texts, and a reconsideration of how teachers'
questioning techniques might enrich rather than impede students'
encounters with difficulty in literary reading.

QUESTIONS ABOUT LITERARY UNDERSTANDING

Any competent reader understands that reading a novel is not the
same as reading a science text. Literature not only informs readers, it
transforms them in subtle or profound ways. Through their encounters
with literature, readers come to know and understand themselves, the
world in which they live, a variety of literary techniques and conventions,
and their own aesthetic experiences. Through these understandings,
they develop identities as individuals, as members of particular communities and cultures, as readers, and as humans, capable of aesthetic appre-

ciation. Thus, the literary "transaction" (Rosenblatt, 1978, 1985) is a multidimensional process, requiring various kinds of understandings.

Self-Understanding

Through the literary experience, readers develop identities as individuals in the world of ideas and people (Holland, 1973, 1975; Petrosky, 1976), and as critical readers in a literary community (Rogers, 1988). As readers make autobiographical associations (Beach, in press; Petrosky, 1981), they discover more about their own growth, as well as their attitudes and beliefs about the world in which they live. As they encounter a variety of texts, they develop the capacity to read critically, discovering their identities within a community of readers. Thus, through their encounters with literature, readers develop as individuals, as social entities, and as literate persons.

Social Understanding

Readers also learn to understand and interpret social and interpersonal relationships (Beach, 1983; Hynds, in press), as well as the norms and conventions of particular cultures (Purves, 1986) relevant to literary works. In understanding the social and cultural context, as well as the factual content of particular literary works, readers are then able to understand the degree to which texts derive or deviate from "real world" phenomena; they learn to distinguish fact from fantasy.

Social knowledge includes not only an understanding of the rules, norms, and expectations of the larger culture, but also the rules and expectations that define what it means to succeed as members of classroom literary communities (Hynds, 1989, in press; Marshall, 1987, 1989). As they participate in classroom discussions, and as they are evaluated in written assignments, readers learn to interpret and understand literature according to the underlying norms and expectations of teachers and peers. Thus, the reading of literature expands and enlarges readers' knowledge of their social world, as well as their understandings of multiple social contexts within which they live and read.

Literary Understanding

Readers must learn to understand a variety of literary conventions for a rich appreciation and interpretation of literature (Beach, 1985; Fish, 1976; Mailloux, 1982; Culler, 1975). Beyond this knowledge, readers also acquire the ability to make intertextual connections (Beach, Appleman, and Dorsey, in press), linking one literary work to another, comparing and contrasting techniques, themes, characterizations, and so forth. Finally, readers must understand what orientation or stance is most appropriate for particular readings (Vipond and Hunt, 1984; Rosenblatt,

1978)—whether to read aesthetically or efferently, for information, for story, or for deeper meaning.

Aesthetic Understanding

Literary texts, as distinct from other types of texts, are both artifact and meaning source. As readers experience literature as aesthetic artifact, they are temporarily able to think "the thoughts of another" (Poulet, 1980: 44) and to become absorbed in the act of reading, rather than other, more peripheral concerns (Rosenblatt, 1978).

WHAT IS SO DIFFICULT ABOUT LITERARY READING?

From a *reading comprehension* viewpoint, readers bring prior knowledge to bear on nonliterary texts in fairly predictable ways. Texts can be classified as more or less "readable" through standardized readability formulas. Readers can be classified as more or less "skilled" by a variety of quantitative tests. Skill hierarchies and levels of thinking can be identified, making it possible to classify teachers' questions and students' responses as "higher" or "lower" on some intellectual scale.

However, there is obviously a certain danger to applying nonliterary models to literary reading. As other essays in this collection argue, literary reading cannot be so easily measured or defined. For one thing, there is never "one ultimate goal" for reading, responding to, or interpreting a literary text. Self-understanding, for instance, is no more or less valid than literary understanding. A point-driven orientation is not superior to a story-driven orientation, though certain stances may be more appropriate for certain literary texts and contexts than others.

Furthermore, literary understandings cannot be developed discretely as a set of skills. Developing a point-driven orientation requires, for instance, more than teaching students to read for meaning or theme. As Vipond, Hunt, Jewett, and Reither (in press) argue, it means teaching readers to read "dialogically"—viewing the text as an intentionally crafted product of an author, attempting to create a particular effect on a reader. This *dialogic* reading requires readers to understand the effects a text has on them, what literary conventions define such effects, how the text comes to mean in terms of their own personal identities, and how the text reflects the values, norms, and expectations of particular cultures.

Further, readers' understandings of what stances are appropriate for particular texts derive from their knowledge of literary conventions, as well as their knowledge of the appropriateness of those stances within their classroom community of readers. Thus, considering the incredible complexity of what it means to "understand" literature, it is important to realize that simply asking "higher order" questions will not automatically

promote the multidimensional insights and emotional responses necessary for a complete encounter with literature. Nor can teachers' questions
be categorized in terms of the degree to which they promote discrete
understandings of self, social relationships, literature, or the aesthetic
experience. Teachers' questions, the way they are presented, the surrounding instructional experiences, and the subliminal messages that
students perceive, all combine to create a particular culture—one that
rewards particular stances, interpretations, and attitudes toward what it
means to "understand" a literary text. Often, this interpretive culture
created by teachers' questions stifles, rather than enlarges, the multiple
and complex understandings essential to the literary experience.

WHAT IS SO DIFFICULT ABOUT CLASSROOM QUESTIONING?

Simplifying Complexity: The Myth of "One Best Response"

Jay, a 12th-grade student, remarks on a former teacher's strategy of
questioning students in order to validate her own preferred response:

> I had this teacher this year who thought that [her idea was the
> only idea] and I didn't get along at all with that teacher.... We
> just sat there and she'd always like [say] "Be quiet" or "pay
> attention."... She had a set idea of what [the interpretation] was
> gonna be and she was gonna tell us. I mean, she tried to get the
> question—she questioned us to try to come up with that idea...
> and that's kinda tough when you're talking about literature.
> [Hynds, 1989]

It is perhaps some small encouragement that, in his twelfth year of
formal schooling, at least Jay was able to show a little awareness that literary texts have more than one correct interpretation. Although it is possible that Jay's teacher intended to help her students to explore ideas
within and beyond the literary text, her questions carried a clear message
that the goal of literary reading was to come up with one acceptable idea,
rather than to play with and explore textual difficulty. Her questioning
techniques apparently served to narrow, rather than broaden, Jay's
response. They drove him away from the interpretive problems that
might have potentially engaged his interest and stimulated his thinking.

The essays in this collection note the unique character of literary
reading to embrace, rather than circumvent, interpretive difficulty (see,
for example, Elam and Adams, this collection). Similarly, Davison, King,
and Kitchener (in press) have noted the difference between, for example, a story problem in arithmetic and the problem of pollution in the real
world. Citing Churchman (1971) and Wood (1983), they contrast "puz-

zles" with what they term "ill-structured problems." Developing "reflective thinking" in individuals, they argue, involves presenting them with *problems* to grapple with, rather than *puzzles* to solve.

Davison and his colleagues challenge teachers to develop "problems for which the student's current assumptions are insufficient and which cause the student to seek more adequate ways of thinking about a problem" (p. 20). By its very indeterminacy, complexity, and relative unfamiliarity, literature presents a whole host of possibilities and interpretive problems for students to explore. The very act of literary reading demands a tolerance of the multiple tensions and disruptions inherent in the literary encounter. As Iser has noted:

> In the oscillation between consistency and "alien associations," between involvement in and observation of the illusion, the reader is bound to conduct his own balancing operation, and it is this that forms to aesthetic experience offered by the literary text. However, if the reader were to achieve a balance, obviously he would then no longer be engaged in the process of establishing and disrupting consistency. . . . In seeking the balance we inevitably have to start out with certain expectations, the shattering of which is integral to the aesthetic experience. [1980: 61]

In the face of this potential discomfort and dissonance, Davison and his associates argue that teachers must "create an atmosphere of thoughtful reasoning . . . [and] acknowledge that the revolutions in thinking that are implied by the Reflective Judgment model are frequently disturbing, frustrating, and even frightening" (p. 20).

Unfortunately, Jay and his teachers have carefully avoided the shattering of illusions and preconceptions so essential to literary reading. Most often, students know that there are a variety of possible interpretations to any literary text, but they implicitly agree to arrive at and conform to the teacher's preferred response in order to succeed in school.

Cathy, a 12th-grade student, has just read "This is My Livingroom" by Tom McAfee. Her somewhat cynical view of teachers and the arbitrariness of their interpretations reveals that she has learned all too well how to play this interpretive game.

I: Do you think that [this story] would be a good story to teach in English class?

C: Well, I think it would be hard because I think everyone would get a different idea. I mean, I don't know where I got the World War I thing. It kinda popped in my head. But I think, if a teacher had gotten the same idea I [did] she would have just kinda made the story fit what she just kinda thought of.

I: So do you think that's a good thing or a bad thing— everybody having a different idea about the story?

C: Well, I think it's harder to teach it if, you know, the more different ideas. It would be okay if the teacher was going to try and accept and develop other people's ideas as well, you know, it wouldn't be like one way that the story goes....

I: How do you feel in a class when everybody seems to have different ideas?

C: Kinda dumb.

I: Does the teacher do anything to kinda make that easier?

C: Well, it depends. If they're [the ideas are] really far-fetched, she'll kinda laugh or say, "Well, I don't think so." But sometimes it seems like she, she tries to make things fit the way she read it. [Hynds, 1989]

Holland (1986) echoes Cathy's dilemma:

At any given moment a teacher may be giving a student hypotheses or hypotheses for finding hypotheses or may be carrying a hypothesis through its testing to sense the return. All these are familiar strategies in teaching. All use the students' responses but seek a homogeneity of response. Typically, this kind of teaching uses only those responses that can be generalized, shared, or otherwise made available to all the students. [p. 444]

In privileging only those responses that can be shared or "made available to all the students," teachers such as the one Cathy describes set up a "least-common denominator" approach to interpretation—one that obliterates the private, idiosyncratic, hypothesis-generating response so essential to literary reading.

Thus, our students are often aware of the need to conform to our often "arbitrarily correct" responses and interpretations of literary texts. When students come to believe that our interpretations are the only ones sanctioned in examinations and other graded projects, our influence on student learning is even more pervasive. Even more disconcerting, however, is that students learn to avoid, rather than to embrace, complexity in literary reading. Notice how these students appear to shy away from literary complexity in classroom reading contexts:

J: In math or science you're doing more actual like activities and problems, or you're doing a lab or something and ah, I mean that's a lot different than trying to figure out why an author

wrote or uses this symbol or wrote what he did. . . . It's more
definite for one thing, because when you're trying to figure out,
I mean even after an English teacher has like, in your class,
come up with why an author wrote something like his, ah, his
motives or whatever... you say "Is that true?" I mean, there's no
definite part about it. [Hynds, 1989]

C: I think like, reading comprehension, for some reason I've
always had a little trouble with it. 'Cause I hate to like try and
think about things. I'd rather just try and read it [the text].
[Hynds, 1989]

Thus, the myth of "one correct response" sets students up to expect
something that does not and *should* not exist in literary reading: an absolute and incontrovertible interpretation. On the contrary, the interpretive
tensions created by competing or alternate explanations are what separate literary from nonliterary reading in the first place. As Iser (1980) has
argued, "the gestalt formation in the reader's consciousness runs counter
to the openness of the text" (p. 334). This very tension, he proposes, is
essential to literary reading. In Iser's terms, the reader's strategies when
confronted with fictional texts "are usually so designed that gestalt formation creates its own latent disturbances" (p. 334).

Similarly, as Perry and Sternberg (1986) have suggested, due to the
often contradictory interpretations suggested by literary texts, readers
must frequently engage in "multiple systems of gap-filling" (p. 314). The
coexistence of conflicting hypotheses in literary reading leads to "heightened perceptibility" (p. 321) on the part of the reader. Although human
beings must rely upon multiple systems of gap-filling in real life, Perry
and Sternberg suggest that typically, only one of two "real life" hypotheses "fits the case, only one of them can be right. . . . In a literary work, on
the other hand, two contradictory hypotheses may both be valid, since
their coexistence may be aesthetically motivated and legitimated in
terms of artistic intentions" (pp. 321–22).

Unfortunately, the interpretive hegemony fostered by many teachers'
questions often disturbs the very tensions and difficulties of interpretation
that make literature truly "literary." The myth of one best response, then,
actually increases the difficulty of literary interpretation by endorsing the
mistaken notion that correct interpretations clearly emerge. This pseudo-
scientific quest for one acceptable response flattens the literary experience, rendering it devoid of its essential complexity and indeterminacy.

Autonomy, Objectivity, and the Myth of the Individual Response

In addition to sidestepping issues of difficulty in literary texts, students are often threatened rather than enriched by the interpretations of

their classmates. Ideally, the classroom community should promote coop-
erative learning, deriving largely from the "intersubjective" responses of
other readers (Bleich, 1986). Class discussions, in the view of most teachers, exist for the purpose of allowing students to compare competing
viewpoints and enrich their own subjective interpretations.

Bleich (1986), for instance, describes the "thought collective in
which individual readings take place: for example, the family, the classroom, the academic meeting" (p. 418). It is in the sharing of readings that
intersubjective interpretations are generated. Citing a number of feminist scholars, Bleich indicts the views of much masculine scholarship that
privileges interpretive objectivity, autonomy, and independence—a view
that runs counter to his collaborative or intersubjective view of reading.

In adhering to this autonomous model of interpretation, teachers'
questions often foster an attitude of competition rather than collaboration, as Hal, a 12th-grade student, poignantly observes:

> When [I'm] in the classroom, like everybody, a lot of times, are
> kind of shy to say something 'cause, you know, it might not be
> right . . . there's been a lot of stuff in my mind this year in
> English class, that we discuss, that I could have said. I just sat
> back and listened to everybody else. [Hynds, 1989]

Thus, teachers' questions within the surrounding context of the
examination or the literature discussion tend to isolate readers and to
make them fearful of a sort of "intellectual plagiarism." Such a viewpoint
tends to make them suspicious, competitive, and, regrettably, often
silenced in each other's presence.

Pseudo-Questions, Trick Questions, and "Beating the System"

Many students seem to believe that in class discussions and literature
assignments, teachers ask "pseudo-questions," rather than questions the
teachers really want to explore. Perhaps because their evaluation methods
are incongruent with their goals of enlarging and privileging readers'
unique responses, teachers are perceived as asking "trick" questions on
examinations, just to determine, at baseline, whether their students have
read the material they have assigned. This minimalistic approach to reading and evaluation does much damage to the way students approach literary texts. Jay remarks on the difficulty of answering such pseudo-questions on a test:

> When I'm reading a book in English I gotta know everything
> that was going on and exactly what was happening because . . .
> because the teachers they come up with these questions that are
> so specific. I mean it's like, I hate quotes on a test. . . . It's like

"who said this and what were they saying when they said this and what was their meaning." ... You might remember it, but you can't put the person's name on it and you ... might not know who said it because of the way it's said, you might not know the context exactly. Because you could have been several places where they could have said it. [Hynds, 1989]

Unfortunately, however, not all students are as astute about the potential arbitrariness of teachers' questions as Jay seems to be. Hal passively accepts his teacher's lack of tolerance for multiple responses in class discussions and tests as one of the hazards of the grading system:

H: Sometimes you might disagree with them [classmates], and then if the teacher agrees with them and you might think that they're right and you're wrong.

I: It's all this "right and wrong" stuff, isn't it?

H: Yeah, I think a lot of it is what you interpret it to be. 'Cause the author, you'll never know if the author meant it, what you interpreted, unless you see him and ask him. So, I think a lot of authors and poets write stuff so everybody can have so many different ways to look at....

I: And so, in light of that, in light of the fact that probably authors try to make multiple meanings out of texts, why do you suppose in schools we often see it the other way around, like there's only one meaning?

H: 'Cause I guess they gotta have some basis for grading and to discuss and they can't keep bringing it, they don't have enough time to go through with it.

I: Do you think that's fair?

H: Oh, not really. But there's nothing anybody could do about it. [Hynds 1989]

When teachers' questions are perceived as purposely tricky—when teachers ask questions with narrow, often meaningless answers—students read with an attitude of "beating the system," or worse yet, like Hal, they feel powerless to succeed, and try to move through the experience as quickly and painlessly as possible.

If Jay's and Hal's comments are any indication, little seems to have changed since 1966, when Louise Rosenblatt first wrote:

To do justice to the text, then, the young reader must be helped to handle his responses to it. Yet the techniques of the usual

English classroom tend to hurry past this process of active creation and re-creation of the text. The pupil is, instead, rushed
into peripheral concerns. How many times youngsters read
poems or stories or plays trying to memorize as many random
details as possible because such "facts" will be the teacher's
means of testing—in multiple answer questions—whether they
have read the work!... Even the search for meaning is reduced
too often to paraphrase that simply dulls and dilutes the impact
of the work.... Our assignments, our ways of testing, our questions about the work, our techniques of analysis, should direct
attention to, not away from, the work as an aesthetic experience.
[Rosenblatt, 1966/1983: 285]

Questioning Levels, Skill Hierarchies, and Reading Processes

Although many of us wish to believe that our questions serve to
teach students to think beyond the text, often our questions seem to
exist for the purpose of creating clear-cut grading distinctions and sepa-
rating "good" from "poor" readers. We think that by asking "higher
level" questions and by leading students through progressively more
difficult levels of thinking, we will help students to master difficult texts.
However, often we succeed only in interfering with our students' natural
meaning-making processes. Judith Langer's poorer readers, for instance,
spent much time in the "being out and stepping into an envisionment"
stance. Langer (1989) argues that "rather than moving 'up' a scale of
abstraction to an 'interpretive' level, students learn to develop a store of
qualitatively different options to use in particular circumstances for particular purposes" (p. 20). Arguing against hierarchical approaches to literary reading, Langer calls for "an alternative to existing category systems
that are primarily based on *types* or *levels* of response" (p. 20).

Cathy is an example of an exceptionally insightful reader, whose
reading processes are greatly disrupted by the pressures of evaluation
and time constraints in classroom examinations and discussions. She
explains:

There's more stuff in my mind [in English class] that I just
haven't had time to sort out.... If I haven't gone over a story or
something really carefully and ... I just haven't sorted it out
enough to deal with it ... and then there's a quiz or something,
I'm like trying to write down everything without answering the
question. [Hynds, 1989]

Cathy's understanding of the text is greatly impaired whenever she is
asked to "step out and move beyond" her envisionment when she is still
trying to step in.

As the comments of these students indicate, teachers' questions in tests and written assignments are frequently indices of students' test-taking ability, rather than their interpretive skills. More than this, such approaches often force students to apprehend literature from a purely cognitive framework, ignoring or suppressing their engagement or affective processes. Thus, such questions often interfere with meaning-making processes and encourage a submissive attitude toward literary reading. All of these influences disable, rather than enable, readers to grapple with interpretive difficulty. Patrick Dias (in press) has recently observed:

> To read and answer someone else's questions is not to read and appropriate the text for oneself. Such an approach inevitably relegates literary reading to the category of school-based activities, dependent on instruction and teacher monitoring to validate it. In such contexts, pupils cannot but read with a "question-answering" schema in mind, a schema derived from past experiences with teachers' questioning procedures, a schema that includes consideration of the subtle verbal and non-verbal cues that signal approval and disapproval. Such an approach is inappropriate for the reading of literature, for the reading of texts for one's own sake, for reading to discover and consider one's own questions. [p. 11]

LITERARY AND NONLITERARY STANCES

The question of what constitutes literature is perhaps as old as the study of literature itself. Classroom curricula organized by historical period seem to reflect the opinion that literature is what "stands the test of time." Modern approaches to secondary literature teaching seem to emanate from the view that adolescent literature is whatever adolescents actually read.

Current theories of literary reading, however, argue the impossibility of defining "literature" apart from a consideration of the dynamic literary transaction. Louise Rosenblatt (1985) has observed that:

> "The reading experts ignore what is usually called "literature," and the "literary" folk, starting with an agreed-upon canon of "literary works," usually ignore the problems of the reading of "ordinary" prose and how it differs from "literary" reading. Each group therefore tends to fall back on seeing "literariness" as inherent in the text, seeking this in content and in syntactic and semantic convention. [p. 101]

Rosenblatt argues that the difference between literary and nonliterary reading "reside[s] in what...is brought to the center of attention and what is pushed into the periphery or ignored" (p. 101). Literary reading, as Rosenblatt defines it, is predominantly "aesthetic." What is brought to the center of attention in reading literary texts is the *immediate experience* of reading, *not* what the reader will take away from that reading at some future time.

Langer (1989) has distinguished literary from nonliterary reading, in that literary reading involves "reaching toward a horizon," rather than "maintaining a point of reference." In reaching toward a horizon, Langer's readers "treated their growing understandings more openly, raising possibilities about the horizon as well as about momentary ideas, focusing on the human situation, seeking to understand interplays between events and emotions and eventualities—toward an understanding of what *might be*" (p. 19). In nonliterary reading, Langer's readers "worked closely, using the topic as a frame of reference, building and refining meanings as they moved toward a more complete understanding of the topic—toward an understanding of what *is*" (p. 19).

Notice how the teacher in the following discussion treats literature in a nonliterary way through a series of fact-oriented questions:

T: Now what kind of things begin to happen as Arthur tries to pull the sword from the stone?

S: He sees everything more clearly.

T: Right, he sees everything more clearly. You were going to say something, Connie?

S: The animals were cheering him on.

T: Yes, the animals do cheer him on. Does anyone know what a gargoyle was?

S: A statue in front of a building.

T: Okay. A gargoyle is like a figure that is supposed to ward off evil spirits. That is my understanding of a gargoyle. Let's look there on page 431.

S: Which column?

T: The second one.

S: If a gargoyle is supposed to ward off evil, then why does it look evil?

T: I'm not sure.

S: If you were a demon wouldn't you go where other demons were?

T: Well, it's like in the second column. Arthur says the sword is fixed, and he tries to pull it out (pointing the students' attention to the text). The animals are actually speaking. This is an example of supernatural that occurs. They all come to cheer Arthur on. Then he finally pulls out the sword. Now, we've always known Arthur was the true king, and Sir Ector now realizes this.

This conversation bears little trace of what Langer terms "reaching toward a horizon." The one glimmer that students may be trying to move beyond the literal meaning of the text (a student's question about gargoyles and evil warding off evil) is quickly overpowered by the teacher's apparent desire to move toward what Langer calls a "point of reference," associated with nonliterary reading: the supernatural events in the story.

As her questioning continues, this teacher reinforces the search for "what *is*" in the text, by drawing attention to the marginal notes and vocabulary terms:

S: This version says the sword was pulled from an anvil.

T: Okay.

S: What is an anvil?

T: An anvil? What is that? What is an anvil used for?

S: That's something a blacksmith uses to...

S: They also always drop an anvil on the roadrunner.

T: Yeah they do. Okay. Look at the picture on 430. It shows the anvil. And Dan, what did you say the blacksmiths use it for?

S: They use it to form nails.

T: To form the nails? Okay. I don't know that much about blacksmiths. So there you have the picture of Arthur pulling the sword from the stone. Now what is it Sir Kay does when Arthur comes back with the sword? We really get a good picture of Sir Kay's character. What does Sir Kay do?

S: He says he pulled it out.

T: Just like Jeff says, Sir Kay tells his father that he pulled it out. Of course he lies. He finally admits the truth on p. 433 in the first column. Sir Ector then gets down on his knee to bow to Arthur, and do you know what condition of the joints Ector has?

S: Gout.

T: Gout. If you look at the bottom of the page, you see it is a condition that causes a painful swelling of the joints.

In this excerpt, students encounter *puzzles* to be solved, and not *problems* to be explored. A superficial discussion of anvils, blacksmiths, and an acute medical condition of the knee appears to undermine and overshadow what might have been an intriguing search for complexities and interpretations. The one hint that the teacher might be moving beyond a peripheral and surface interpretation—her comment about Sir Kay's character—is quickly overtaken by a question about Sir Ector's gout.

Thus, at least in this excerpt, compelling human issues—the struggle between love and power, goodness and evil, honor and dishonor—are apparently lost in the search for some very literal information. In attempting to *reduce* the difficulty of this text, the teacher has actually *created* a far more serious difficulty: training her students to approach a literary text in a nonliterary way.

In his recent examination of the patterns of talk in six secondary classrooms, Marshall (1989) concluded that:

> We seldom . . . found evidence that discussions were moving toward a point where teachers could remove themselves, disappear, and "watch it happen." We seldom saw evidence that students were moving much beyond answering their teachers' questions (however carefully these questions may have been framed). Rather, the general pattern seemed to be one of students' contributing to an interpretive agenda implied by those questions. . . . While the goal expressed by teachers was to help students toward a point where they could individually develop a reasoned response to the text, we observed few occasions where students could practice such interpretive skills—at least during large-group discussions. [pp. 41–42]

TEXTBOOK ANSWERS AND LITERARY UNDERSTANDING

One look at most current literature anthologies reveals how classroom questions, by attempting to reduce and make manageable the difficulty in literary texts, potentially reinforce and compound this difficulty. Notice the following excerpt of the discussion questions following an anthologized version of Jack London's "To Build a Fire":

1. (a) What is the setting in this story? (b) What details in the early part of the story make you aware of the intense cold? (c) Why is the setting important?

2. Review the handbook article on narrative point of view (page 558). (a) What point of view does Jack London use to tell this story? (b) Why do you think he uses this point of view?

3. (a) What advice was given by the old-timer at Sulpher Creek? (b) What was the man's reaction to this advice before he started on his journey?

4. Each of the references below has to do with the man's attitude toward his situation. Locate each reference and explain the attitudes expressed in the passage.

   (a) page 404, column 1, paragraph 1

   (b) page 407, column 2, paragraph 1

Six additional pages and paragraphs are listed (in *Counterpoint in Literature*, Scott, Foresman, 1976).

Readers often begin interpretations by making sense of the text in light of their own personal experiences/identifications. However, the questions in this textbook make little use of students' personal responses or meaning-making processes. They begin, not from the reader's initial response, but from a minor point within the text, by asking students to comment on the setting of the story. There is no open invitation to explore initial idiosyncratic responses. There is no mention of readers' engagement or feelings while reading the story.

The only reference to social understanding in this set of questions concerns the hero's "attitude" toward certain story events. One major difficulty with this question is the way in which students are asked to reconstruct piecemeal perceptions of the main character. Short-answer questions such as "Locate each reference and explain the attitudes expressed in the passage" have been found to be less effective in encouraging literary interpretation (Marshall, 1987) than no questions at all, in that they fragment the reading process and preclude holistic meaning-making.

The questions about point of view are obviously designed to elicit students' knowledge of literary technique. Unfortunately, these decontextualized and seemingly pointless questions do little to help students to make the sort of "reading-writing" connections they were intended to develop. There is no apparent reason (other than demonstrating mastery to a teacher) for these questions. Students are not expected to experiment with third-person narration (as opposed to first-person) in their own writing. Asking them to check a handbook only further removes this activity from any real reading-writing context they might encounter.

As the previous comments of Ken, Jay, Cathy, and Hal indicate, study questions or textbook questions such as these often interfere with the aesthetic involvement and exploratory stance so necessary to literary reading. Whether questions are used before or after a reading experience, students have learned all too well the "skill" of marking places in the text and memorizing textual trivia. Such strategies often interfere with the very meaning-making processes they were intended to foster. When reading is taught as a "study skill," rather than an encounter with a text of potential significance, then literary reading takes on a difficulty far beyond the difficulty of basic comprehension and inference.

Thus, textbook and study questions often force students inside the text before they have had a chance to enter into an envisionment; they fragment the interpretive process into a consideration of individual aspects of the work, rather than the whole; they lead students away from the literary experience and into an auxiliary handbook or into preselected places in the text; they focus on literal fact-finding, rather than complex or personal meaning-making. Finally, such questions are often posed for no apparent purpose, except to convince the teacher or some other adult that the student has read and "understood" the selection.

As Brody, DeMilo, and Purves (1989) have observed in their assessment of current standardized literature tests and textbook examinations in the United States:

> The imaginative power of literature and the power of literature to capture the imagination and intellect of the reader remain unexplored in most of these assessments, which treat the texts as if they were no different from articles in encyclopedias. Under these conditions, it would seem difficult for students to see literature as anything but dead and lifeless; this view of literature is perpetuated by the most potent force in the curriculum, the test. [p. 30]

DIFFICULT QUESTIONS AND QUESTIONS OF DIFFICULTY

Ideally, teachers' questions should guide and support students as they move toward their own interpretive horizons. Frequently, however, teachers' questions fragment, flatten, objectify, and distract from the literary experience. Such questions invite students to prove that they have read and understood a text, rather than to explore a multitude of interpretations and possibilities.

Through their questions, teachers often unwittingly isolate readers from the classroom collective, privilege competition rather than collaboration, mystify the interpretive process, at the same time as they reduce it to the search for one right answer. More than this, teachers' questions typically place interpretive authority squarely in the hands of the teacher. Through class discussions and examinations, teachers' questions usually encourage intellectual passivity that impoverishes students and limits their ability to create a unique, personal, tentative, exploratory response.

Our questions should provide a framework that leads students to their *own* questions, laying open the vast horizon of possibilities, not closing it down, inviting students to ask questions of themselves and of each other. We should ask questions that are knowledge-producing, not knowledge-reproducing, a by-product of our *own* ongoing inquiry, not a residue of fixed and preformulated conclusions. Most importantly, our questions should give way to silent reflection at least as often as immediate articulation. Wolfgang Iser (1971) has said that "literature simulates life, not in order to portray it, but in order to allow the reader to share in it" (p. 44). The same could be said of teachers' questions and literary interpretation. Questions should exist, not to *portray* literature, but to invite readers to *share* in it. And in that questioning and sharing of experience, students and teachers become empowered to embrace the difficulties and complexities unique to literary reading.

REFERENCES

Beach, R. (1983). "Attitudes, social conventions, and response to literature." *Journal of Research and Development in Education*, 16, 47–53.

———. (1985). "Discourse conventions and researching response to literary dialogue." In C. Cooper, ed., *Researching response to literature and the teaching of literature*. Norwood, N.J.: Ablex.

———. (1990). "The creative development of meaning: Using autobiographical experiences to interpret literature." In S. Straw and D. Bogdan, eds., *Beyond communication: Reading comprehension and criticism*. Upper Montclair, N.J.: Heinemann/Boynton/Cook.

Beach, R., Appleman, D., and Dorsey, S. (1990). "Secondary students' evolving knowledge of literature: A study of intertextual links." In R. Beach and S. Hynds, eds. *Becoming readers and writers during adolescence and adulthood*. Norwood, N.J.: Ablex.

Bleich, D. (1986). "Intersubjective reading." *New literary history*, 27 (3), 401–21.

Brody, P., DeMilo, C., and Purves, A. C. (1989). *The Current State of Assessment in Literature*. (Report no. 3.1). Albany: Center for the Learning and Teaching of Literature.

Churchman, C. W. (1971). *The design of inquiring systems: Basic concepts of systems and organizations*. New York: Basic Books.

Culler, J. (1975). *Structuralist poetics*. Ithaca: Cornell University Press.

Davison, M. L., King, P. M., and Kitchener, K. S. (1990). "Developing reflective thinking and writing." In R. Beach and S. Hynds, eds.

Developing Discourse Practices in Adolescence and Adulthood. Norwood, N.J.: Ablex.

Dias, P. (1990). "A literary response perspective on teaching reading comprehension." In S. Straw and D. Bogdan, eds., *Beyond Communication: Comprehension and criticism.* Upper Montclair, N.J.: Heinemann/Boynton/Cook.

Fish, S. (1976). "Interpreting the variorum." *Critical Inquiry,* 2, 465–85.

Herber, H. L. (1967). *Teaching reading in content areas.* Englewood Cliffs, N.J.: Prentice-Hall.

Holland, N. (1973). *Poems in persons.* New York: W. W. Norton.

———. (1975). *Five readers reading.* New Haven: Yale University Press.

———. (1986). "The miller's wife and the professors: Questions about the transactive theory of reading." *New Literary History,* 27, 422–47.

Hynds, S. (1985). "Interpersonal cognitive complexity and the literary response processes of adolescent readers." *Research in the Teaching of English,* 19, 386–402.

———. (1989). "Bringing life to literature and literature to life: Social constructs and contexts of four adolescent readers." *Research in the Teaching of English.*

———. (1990). "Reading as a social event: Comprehension and response in the text, classroom, and world." In S. Straw and D. Bogdan, eds., *Beyond communication: Comprehension and criticism.* Upper Montclair, N.J.: Heinemann/Boynton/Cook.

Iser, W. (1971). "Indeterminacy and the reader's response in prose fiction." In J. H. Miller, (ed.) *Aspects of Narrative: Selected papers from the English Institute.* New York: Columbia University Press, 1–45.

———. (1980). "Texts and readers." *Discourse Processes,* 3, 327–43.

Langer, J. A. (1985). "Levels of questioning: An alternative view." *Reading Research Quarterly,* 10, 586–602.

———. (1989). *The process of understanding literature* (Report no. 2.1). Albany, N.Y.: Center for the Learning and Teaching of Literature.

Mailloux, S. (1982). *Interpretive conventions: The reader in the study of American fiction.* Ithaca: Cornell University Press.

Manzo, A. V. (1970). "Reading and questioning: The re-quest procedure." *Reading Improvement,* 7, 80–83.

Marshall, J. D. (1987). "The effects of writing on students' understanding of literary texts." *Research in the Teaching of English*, 21, 30–63.

———. (1989). *Patterns of discourse in classroom discussions of literature.* (Report no. 2.9). Albany, N.Y.: The Center for the Learning and Teaching of Literature.

Perry, M., and Sternberg, M. (1986). "The king through ironic eyes: Biblical narrative and the literary reading process." *Poetics Today*, 7, 275–322.

Petrosky, A. (1976). "The effects of reality perception and fantasy on response to literature." *Research in the Teaching of English*, 10, 239–58.

———. (1981). "From story to essay: Reading and writing." *College Composition and Communication*, 33, 19–36.

Poulet, G. (1980). In J. P. Tompkins, ed. *Reader-response criticism: From formalism to post-structuralism.* Baltimore: Johns Hopkins University Press.

Purves, A. C. (1986). "Cultural literacy and research in response to literature." Paper presented at the annual NCTE assembly on research conference, Chicago.

Raphael, T. E., and Pearson, P. D. (1982). *The effects of metacognitive strategy awareness training on students' question answering behavior.* Urbana: University of Illinois, Center for the Study of Reading.

Rogers, T. (1988). "Students as literary critics: The interpretive theories, processes, and experiences of ninth-grade students." Dissertation, University of Illinois.

Rosenblatt, L. M. (1978). *The reader, the text, the poem: A transactional theory of the literary work.* Carbondale: Southern Illinois University Press.

———. (1983). *Literature as exploration.* New York: Modern Language Association.

———. (1985). "Viewpoints: Transaction versus interaction—a terminological rescue operation." *Research in the Teaching of English*, *19*, 97–107.

Stauffer, R. G. (1959). "A directed reading-thinking plan." *Education*, 79, 527–32.

———. (1969). *Directing reading maturity as a cognitive process.* New York: Harper and Row.

Vipond, D., and Hunt, R. A. (1984). "Point-driven understanding: Pragmatic and cognitive dimensions of literary reading." *Poetics*, 13, 261–77.

Vipond, D., Hunt, R. A., Jewett, J., and Reither, J. A. (1990). "Making sense of reading." In R. Beach and S. Hynds, eds., *Becoming readers and writers in adolescence and adulthood.* Norwood, N.J.: Ablex.

Wood, P.K. (1983). "Inquiring systems and problem structure: Implications for cognitive development." *Human Development,* 26, 249–65.

7.

*Making it Hard: Curriculum and Instruction as Factors in the Difficulty of Literature**

Martin Nystrand

The difficulty of any work of literature, the authors in this series agree, cannot be adequately explained by text features alone. Following Stanley Fish (1980), Purves (in this volume) argues that literature education is essentially a process of aesthetic socialization, or enculturation into the interpretive community of those who read, understand, and value accepted works of literature. This acquired ability superficially entails, as Hirsch (1987) argues concerning cultural literacy, a passing familiarity with those texts considered literary. More fundamentally, it entails particular values, tastes, and mannerisms empowering particular responses and motivating particular sorts of readings—namely, poetic, aesthetic readings (Rosenblatt, 1978). The difficulty of any given work of literature, then, is not categorical—that is, for all time and all readers; nor is it fully a matter of such text characteristics as syntax and lexis. Rather, the difficulty of any particular literary text ultimately depends on the standards that the literary community establishes in treating and interpreting it. As Purves concludes, "A text's difficulty depends upon the nature of the understanding expected" (p. 167).

Touponce, citing Barthes, Derrida, and Lacan, comes to a similar conclusion. He argues that it is the nature of interpretation in any given case that determines the difficulty of the text, for it is the nuance of individual readings that breathes life and meaning—simple, complicated, or otherwise—into the text. Hence, understanding the difficulty of any given text requires looking beyond the text itself to the actual readings of the text, just as understanding reading-practices involves looking

*The author is grateful for counsel and advice on this research by Adam Gamoran, and appreciates the research assistance of Mark Berends, Dae-dong Hahn, and John Knapp, as well as the contributions of the teachers and students who participated in the study reported in this chapter.

beyond individual reading skills to the institutions that educate the readers. "In other words," writes Touponce, "the theory of the text suggests that the idea of difficulty is less a property of texts themselves than of the ways in which institutions train us to read" (p. 53).

For Elam, difficulty is endemic to textuality itself. Language is never transparent, and there is no definitive account of the meaning of any given text. Rather, the act of reading itself constitutes meaning, and it is the nature of reading to complicate the text, to introduce difficulty. "Any reading that . . . contemplates not what it knows but how it can come to know anything at all, will take us rapidly from certainty to uncertainty, from sure answers to unanswerable questions, from stable centers to disappearing lines and dislocated boundaries" (p. 76). For Elam, difficulty is an aspect not of text but rather of thinking about text. Nor, she contends, is this difficulty undesirable, something ideally if not unfeasibly to be removed through assiduous study. But she acknowledges that the challenge for education is to make difficult texts accessible without oversimplifing them.

From a different perspective, Hazard Adams (in this volume) argues that a text is difficult when readers are not sufficiently well educated to take up its demands. This is why, he contends, late twentieth-century students of literature often have a hard time with classical allusions and important facets of classical and even modern literature; they have no understanding of Latin and Greek, or of literary traditions, and a very superficial sense of history, literary or otherwise.

In his analysis of text readability, Chafe (in this volume) shows how even sources of difficulty ostensibly located in the text actually originate beyond the text. Key to the difference in readability between two texts he analyzes—a comparatively easy passage from Edith Wharton and a more obscure passage from Henry James—is the relative discrepancy between the world of the text and reader knowledge. James is a more difficult author for modern readers than Wharton partly because he makes more obscure references for these readers than does Wharton. As I have noted elsewhere (Nystrand, 1986), shared knowledge and well-managed reciprocity between writer and reader are a hallmark of all readable texts. As a result, readability is not categorical and cannot be determined from examination of text features alone; readability potentially changes with every new group of readers, who, along with the author and text, configure the textual space, or semantic potential, of the communication between them.

If difficulty in literature involves more than the text itself, what are the implications of this conclusion for curriculum and instruction? Clearly, in choosing literary titles of appropriate difficulty, teachers must consider more than the texts themselves. It makes no sense to talk definitively of the inherent difficulty of *The Grapes of Wrath* or *Animal Farm* or any other text, for any given work of literature will vary in difficulty for students depending on the students' abilities and predispositions, as well as what teachers and their students actually do with it. *Animal Farm* is a relatively easy book when read simply as an animal story; it is comparatively more difficult when treated in depth as an allegory. In short, curriculum and instruction—what teachers ask students to do—are themselves significant factors in the difficulty of any work of literature studied in school. In understanding the pedagogical difficulty of literature, it is consequently appropriate to inquire about just which sorts of practices complicate, and just which sorts of practices enhance, literature understanding and achievement.

In her paper, Hynds (in this volume) begins to examine research on curriculum and instruction from this point of view. For example, she notes that Gall (1984) found that 20 percent of teacher questions are procedural, 60 percent seek to elicit recall, and only 20 percent require analysis. She notes that Hoetker and Ahlbrand (1969) found that literature teachers typically ask a question every twelve seconds or less, a dizzying pace that would indeed seem to favor recall over higher order thinking. In a study of 58 eighth-grade literature classes of varied abilities and socio-economic status, Nystrand and Gamoran (1989) found less than a minute per day devoted to discussion and small-group work. Only 11 percent of the teachers' questions in these classes involved *uptake*, in which teachers incorporated previous student answers into subsequent questions, and only 12 percent of their questions were *authentic*, meaning that for almost all their questions teachers were looking for particular answers. What effects do such practices as these have on students' understandings of and responses to literature? Do they facilitate or complicate learning? And just what sorts of learning do they promote?'

A STUDY OF THE INSTRUCTIONAL CORRELATES OF
LITERATURE ACHIEVEMENT

To examine these issues, I reexamined the data noted above (Nystrand and Gamoran, 1989) for instructional correlates of difficulty of recall, on the one hand, and difficulty of depth of understanding, on the other. In other words, I sought to distinguish instructional practices that complicate recall from those that make it difficult for students to understand literature in depth.

In our study, we distinguished two sorts of student engagement: "procedural," which concerns observance of classroom rules and regulations, and "substantive," which involves sustained commitment to the content and issues of academic study. We found empirical support for the hypothesis that substantive, but not procedural, engagement bears a strong relationship to literature achievement. In other words, merely doing homework, paying attention in class, and answering questions were not enough to assure that our subjects might do well on our measure of literature achievement. Significantly, literature achievement seems not to be well explained in terms of student behavior alone. Rather, substantive achievement seems best explained in terms of a comprehensive instructional context distinguished by extensive interaction between students and teacher, including: (a) numerous authentic teacher questions—that is, questions such as open-ended ones for which teachers do not prespecify answers; (b) discussion of literature in terms of students' own experience; (c) uptake—that is, the incorporation of previous student answers into subsequent teacher questions; (d) deliberate relation of individual works to other readings; and (e) ample time for discussion.

Measure of Literature Achievement

The literature test used as the dependent variable in our analysis consisted of a set of questions concerning five literature titles students had studied during eighth grade; the test was administered at the end of this grade in the spring. Four of these titles were chosen as a stratified sample representing the kinds of literature each class had studied; if half the titles studied were short stories, then two of the four were short stories. The fifth selected title was the one work the class had spent the most time on; typically it was either a novel, such as *To Kill a Mockingbird* or *A Tale of Two Cities*, or a drama, such as *Romeo and Juliet*. Only short stories, novels, and dramas were selected.

The test involved a set of increasingly more probing questions, ranging from naming or describing as many characters from each story as students could remember and explaining the ending of each story, to outlining the themes and conflicts of each and relating theme, conflict, and ending. Students were asked to elaborate on these especially for the one title on which their class had spent the most time (i.e., the fifth selection). All students answered the same general questions though the details of each test varied depending on the titles studied and selected.

Scoring

These tests were read at least twice by trained graduate students from the Department of English at the University of Wisconsin-Madison. Each test was scored for: (a) extent of recall; (b) depth of understanding; (c) number of endings remembered; (d) relation of ending to denouement; (e) relation of conflict or ending to theme; (f) understanding the internal motivations of characters; (g) interpretive treatment of the major selection; and (h) level of discourse used to discuss theme and conflict.

Readers read the entire test and then determined a single, holistic score for each of the items listed above. Each student's literature score derived from this test was the sum of each of the components listed above. The overall reliability of the assessment, computed as a correlation of the two readings, was $r = .90$.

Subjects

In all, 1,041 students in 58 eighth-grade English classes in 16 Midwestern schools participated in this study. Three of these schools were rural and all white; four were suburban, mostly white, and mostly upper-middle class; and nine were urban composed of students representing mixed socio-economic and ethnic backgrounds.

Other Data Sources

Data sources included student tests, teacher and student questionnaires concerning instructional practices and student backgrounds, and class observations. Each class was observed four times, twice in the fall and twice in the spring. The main purpose of the observations was to flesh out the portrait of instructional practices provided by the questionnaires.

Control Measures

In the fall of data collection, students completed two tasks that were used as control measures in the study. One of these consisted of two brief stories and one poem from the National Assessment of Educational Progress; students were required to read the selections, answer multiple-choice test items, and write a page in response to one of the stories. This test served as a control of literature ability. The other control measure was a writing sample in which students wrote a brief personal essay.

In addition to these two measures, our study was controlled for race, ethnicity, sex, socio-economic status, and eighth grade, since a few of our schools placed some seventh graders in eighth-grade classes.

SOME HYPOTHESES CONCERNING THE EFFECTS OF INSTRUCTIONAL PRACTICES ON (A) DIFFICULTY OF RECALL AND (B) DIFFICULTY OF UNDERSTANDING IN DEPTH

In the data we collected, recall and depth of understanding correlate rather substantially ($r = .707$). This is no surprise, of course, since recall is surely a prerequisite to understanding in depth, and depth of understanding surely enhances recall. But the two cognitive processes are not the same (indeed, the possibility of understanding in depth without comparable recall may well provide a charitable explanation for the phenomenon of professorly absentmindedness!). In our study, we measured extent of recall in terms of factual information and extensiveness of detail that students produced concerning the five titles listed on the test. By contrast, our measure of depth of understanding required gauging the extent to which students had integrated these same details and information into an interpretive framework.

We would expect procedural engagement to be an essential prerequisite for both extent of recall and depth of understanding, since doing one's work is the sine qua non of all school learning. Related to this, we would obviously expect outright disengagement, such as failing to do homework, to complicate both recall and understanding in depth, since such failure must irrevocably increase the difficulty of both.

Many experimental studies in psychology show generally that the manipulation or elaboration of material being studied tends to improve recall and learning. Applebee (1984) and Langer and Applebee (1987) show how writing—including note-taking, answering short-answer questions, summary writing, and essay writing—specifically provide for such processing. Hence, we would expect recall and depth of understanding to be made difficult to the extent that writing is minimal and perfunctory. We should expect similar, negative results for minimal class discussion of readings. Conversely, we should expect comprehension and recall to improve when teachers help students to relate individual texts to their previous readings, previous class discussions, and topics they have written about. We should, furthermore, expect uptake to enhance comprehension and recall, for by following up on the responses of their students, teachers increase the extent to which students reflect on and process their thoughts.

Clearly, there is a trade-off between depth of treatment and coverage of material (Newmann, 1988), and in this respect, we might expect instruction that focuses exclusively on recall to be at odds with understanding in depth. For example, one characteristic of recitation devoted to recall of previously learned material is a relatively quick pace, which is consistent, on the one hand, with the 5.2 question per minute pace that Hoetker and Ahlbrand (1969) report for literature instruction, and the 3:1 ratio of recall to higher order questions that Gall (1984) reports, on the other. (The classes we observed were characterized by a slower pace: 3.23 questions per minute on average with a minimum of 1.51 and a maximum of 9.33.)

If depth of understanding, unlike recall, requires an agile, proficient interpretive framework, then effective instruction must clearly foster the development of such a framework; specifically it must promote reflection and thoughtfulness. Langer and Applebee (1987), for example, distinguish essays and extended writing from short-answer exercises in just this way, the former fostering depth of understanding and the latter enhancing recall.

One reason that notes, short-answer questions, and summary writing promote recall but not depth of understanding is that they deal not with the student's but rather with someone else's ideas and information. Unlike recall, depth of understanding requires the individual learner's elaboration of an interpretive framework. It is an important purpose of authentic discourse to promote just such development. When teachers ask authentic questions—eliciting responses and opinions and encouraging individual interpretations—they open the floor to student ideas for examination, elaboration, reconsideration, and revision. When teachers help students read literature on their own terms and values, reading also becomes authentic and serves a similar cognitive function. In Rosenblatt's (1938) terms, there is an interaction between the world of the reader and the world of the text. In Smith's (1971) terms, comprehension is enhanced when, working from a store of personal knowledge, the reader is able more easily to predict the information of the text.

In our research, we code questions as *authentic* if they are genuinely open-ended or if they have no prespecified answers. Authentic questions allow students considerable input into discussion. By contrast, test questions (inauthentic questions for which the teacher is looking for particular answers) allow students no input into the course of the discussion, since the agenda for questions and answers is set by the teacher before the class even begins. Hence, "What is the conflict in Act I?" is a test question if the teacher has a particular answer in mind. By contrast, "What do you think the author is trying to do here?" is authentic if the teacher is receptive to the student's opinion and does not insist on any one particular answer.

Why should authentic discourse promote depth of understanding? First, the character and tone of classroom discourse set important expectations for learning. When teachers ask genuine questions about what students are thinking (and not just to see if they have done their homework), they promote fundamental expectations for learning by treating students seriously as thinkers—that is, by indicating that what students think is interesting and indeed worth examining.In effect, they treat each student *as a primary source of information,* thereby giving them all an opportunity to deal with things in their own frames of reference. Authentic questions prominently underscore the character of instruction where students are "major players" in the forum of the classroom, where communication is not a one-way affair, and consequently where the terms of reciprocity between teachers and their students are upheld not merely in procedures but in substance as well.

RESULTS

We can best consider these hypotheses by examining the instructional variables noted above in terms of difficulty of recall, on the one hand, and difficulty of depth of understanding, on the other.

Before doing this, however, it is useful to examine the types and extent of writing that characterized classes in our study, as well as extent of discussion, uptake, and authentic questions. This information is provided in Table 1.

About 85 percent of the students in our sample completed both their writing and reading tasks.On average they spent just less than an hour a week on homework. In class, more than 34 percent actively participated in question-and-answer, and students rarely failed to answer questions.

Yet only about 12 percent of teacher questions were authentic, and just 11 percent of all teacher questions involved uptake. Less than a minute a day was, on average, devoted to class discussion. As Nystrand and Gamoran (1989: 19) note, "the overall picture appears highly consistent with earlier descriptions of secondary school classrooms as orderly but lifeless (Sizer, 1984; Goodlad, 1984; Powell, Farrar, and Cohen, 1985)." Specifically looking at writing, we find that the most frequent type of writing was short-answer; such extensive types as paragraph-length and more were clearly less frequent. According to teacher report, students in our study, on average, wrote more than a page less than twice a month. By contrast, they completed short-answer exercises nearly eight times a month. These results are consistent with those in Applebee's (1981) study of writing in American high schools.

To explore these hypotheses, *difficulty of recall* was computed as the opposite of recall (i.e., -1 x RECALL), and *difficulty of depth of understanding* was computed as the opposite of depth of understanding (i.e., -1 x DEPTH). Table 2 presents two regression analyses in which difficulty of recall and difficulty of depth of understanding served as the dependent variables, to be explained by variation in background and instruction. In both analyses, instructional variables are controlled for background and prior writing and reading abilities.

I have suggested that recall and depth are irrevocably complicated by students' failure to do their work. This prediction is partly supported by the analysis in Table 2, showing that failing to complete writing tasks significantly increased the difficulty of both recall and depth of understanding. In addition, failure to answer teacher questions increased difficulty of depth of understanding.

Beyond this, I suggested that recall and depth of understanding should significantly depend on extent of manipulation and elaboration of information. Table 2 provides ample support for this hypothesis. Both

Table 1. Means and Standard Deviations of Variables Included in Regression Analyses. (N = 924 students)

Variable	Mean	Standard Deviation
TEST SCORES		
Recall on spring literature test	1.917	.876
Depth of understanding	1.212	.120
Fall reading	21.620	.311
Fall writing	6.412	1.388
BACKGROUND		
Sex (1 = female)	.508	.500
Race (1 = black)	.090	.286
Ethnicity (1 = Hispanic)	.102	.303
SES	.016	.825
Grade (1 = eighth)	.879	.327
PROCEDURAL VARIABLES		
% reading not completed	15.722	22.913
% writing not completed	13.205	12.217
% nonresponse to questions	2.526	3.297
% active in class	34.441	21.884
Time on homework[1]	.957	1.069
INSTRUCTIONAL VARIABLES		
Quantity of writing (weighted score)	1.527	.284
Freq. short-answer questions[2]	7.834	4.442
Freq. write at least a paragraph[2]	5.633	5.201
Freq. write essays: 2 paragraphs or more[2]	2.066	3.173
Freq. write at least 1 page[2]	1.751	2.975
% teacher questions authentic	23.487	13.265
% reading tasks judged authentic by students	20.235	12.219
% questions exhibiting uptake	11.030	7.348
Contiguity of reading[2]	10.658	2.752
Discussion time[3]	.770	1.716

[1]hrs/week
[2]times per month
[3]minutes/day

recall and depth of understanding were made difficult in classes where students did little writing. Both recall and depth of understanding were enhanced by uptake and complicated by its absence. Recall specifically improved to the extent that classes related individual texts to other things they had read. Depth of understanding, moreover, significantly depended on amount of discussion.

Table 2. Effects of Classroom Variables on Literature Performance

Effects of frequency of, quantity of, authenticity of, participation in, and contiguity of writing, reading, and classroom talk on difficulty of recall and difficulty of understanding literature in depth. Metric regression coefficients, with standard errors in parentheses. (N = 762 students, missing values deleted)

	Difficulty of Recall	*Difficulty of Understanding in Depth*
BACKGROUND VARIABLES		
Grade (1 = eighth)	.054	-.183
	(.090)	(.118)
Race (1 = black)	.246****	.068
	(.091)	(.120)
Ethnicity (1 = Hispanic)	.122	.165
	(.089)	(.117)
SES	-.107****	-.138***
	(.036)	(.048)
Sex (1 = female)	-.120**	-.174*
	(.052)	(.069)
Fall writing	-.073****	-.105****
	(.021)	(.027)
Fall reading	-.034****	-.036****
	(.005)	(.007)
PROCEDURAL VARIABLES		
Time on homework	-.065***	-.058*
	(.024)	(.031)
Reading not completed	.0004	.0004
	(.002)	(.003)
Writing not completed	.005**	.002**
	(.002)	(.003)
Participation in class	-.001	-.001
	(.002)	(.002)
No response to teacher questions	.008	.026*
	(.010)	(.013)
INSTRUCTIONAL VARIABLES		
Amount of writing	-.256**	-.289**
	(.104)	(.137)
Discussion time	-.022	-.038*
	(.016)	(.022)
Authenticity of teacher questions	-.0005	-.006**
	(.002)	(.003)
Authenticity of readings	-.003	-.018***
	(.005)	(.006)

	Difficulty of Recall	Difficulty of Understanding in Depth
INSTRUCTIONAL VARIABLES		
Uptake	-.015****	-.020****
	(.005)	(.006)
Relating discussions to		
other discussions and	.005	.001
student compositions	(.004)	(.005)
Relating readings to other readings	-.046**	-.018
	(.019)	(.025)
R-SQUARE	.353	.339

*p < .10
**p < .05
***p < .01
****p < .001

Table 3. Effects of Writing on Literature Performance

Effects of selected modes of writing on difficulty of recall and difficulty of understanding literature in depth. Metric regression coefficients, with standard errors in parentheses. (N = 1,031 students, missing values deleted)

	Difficulty of Recall	Difficulty of Understanding in Depth
BACKGROUND VARIABLES		
Grade (1 = eighth)	-.100	-.299***
	(.075)	(.101)
Race (1 = black)	.437****	.242**
	(.081)	(.108)
Ethnicity (1 = Hispanic)	.232***	.233**
	(.083)	(.110)
SES	-.166****	-.199***
	(.031)	(.042)
Sex (1 = female)	-.055	-.098*
	(.048)	(.064)
Fall writing	-.106****	-.151****
	(.019)	(.025)
Fall reading	-.047****	-.048****
	(.005)	(.006)
TYPE OF WRITING		
Freq. of short-answer exercises	.015**	.024***
	(.007)	(.009)
Freq. of writing at	-.014**	-.019**
least a paragraph	(.006)	(.008)

Table 3. (continued)

	Difficulty of Recall	Difficulty of Understanding in Depth
TYPE OF WRITING		
Freq. of writing	-.038****	-.058****
1 page or more	(.010)	(.013)

*p < .10
**p < .05
***p < .01
****p < .001

Table 3 examines in some detail the effects of different sorts of writing on difficulty of both recall and depth of understanding. As predicted, frequency of extensive writing enhanced both recall and depth of understanding. Specifically, frequent paragraph-length writing improved both recall and depth. Page-length writing was even more effective; comparing the coefficients for recall and depth shows that frequently writing one page or more is about 2.7 times more beneficial than frequently writing at least a paragraph; for depth the ratio is about 3.3. By contrast, frequently completing short-answer exercises in fact degraded recall and depth of understanding. Applebee (1984) offers one explanation for this surprising result. He notes that, because writing best assists learning of the topics it is focused on, such narrow-banded activities as short-answer exercises are likely to interfere with total recall. In addition, we might also speculate on the possibility of students' completing these exercises, albeit poorly, without having actually read the material involved.

Finally, I argued that depth of understanding, unlike recall, benefits from authentic instructional discourse. In its absence, we should expect students to have difficulty in this regard. Table 2 provides support for this distinction as well. Unlike recall, depth of understanding was significantly enhanced by both authenticity of teacher questions and authenticity of readings; both of these declined to the extent that either or both are absent.

DISCUSSION

This study demonstrates, first, that curriculum and instruction significantly affect the difficulty or ease that students experience with literature. Specifically we find empirical support for the contention of all the authors in this volume that literature difficulty is more than a matter of which texts are taught; it is also a matter of how they are taught—that is, instruction.

Generally, literature will be difficult for students for obvious reasons, such as their failure to complete tasks and answer teacher questions. Uptake is important to both recall and depth of understanding. Of all the instructional variables examined in this study, however, the most notable is writing. The absence of frequent, extensive writing was by far the most significant factor in handicapping recall and understanding. By comparing coefficients in Table 2, we can see that quantity of writing positively affects both recall and depth of understanding much more than the amount of time spent on homework. Specifically, increasing writing assignments by merely one paragraph (i.e., asking students to write two paragraphs instead of one or three paragraphs instead of two) increases recall by .256 points. Compared to this, increasing homework by one hour a week results in a mere .065 point increase in recall. Of course, if students write regularly and extensively, they no doubt do lots of homework. Hence, the import of this finding is to underscore the importance of regularly assigning written homework.

We also find that different instructional practices potentially complicate literature in different ways. Recall is sensitive to the extent to which teachers help students relate their readings to other readings and also to previous things students have written. If we were to derive a hypothetical high school literature class from the data of this study devoted exclusively to recall, it might be as follows. The teacher would assign homework regularly that would be completed by all the students. This homework would involve frequent paragraph- and page-length writing. Little if any of this writing would involve short-answer exercises. In class, the teacher would lead discussions that regularly alluded to this writing, and also to previously studied literature selections. The teacher would regularly follow up on students' responses by asking them further questions.

If, on the other hand, we were to derive a hypothetical high school literature class devoted exclusively to depth of understanding, it might be as follows. The teacher would assign homework regularly that would be completed by all the students. This homework would involve frequent paragraph- and page-length writing. Little if any of this writing would involve short-answer exercises. Class time would be characterized by lots of uptake and authentic questions probing student responses and understandings of their readings. Discussion, wherein students regularly comment on each other's responses without prompting by the teacher, would be common. The teacher would take care to help students see relations between the narrative worlds of the works they read and their own individual experiences. We should point out that this latter class designed to promote depth of understanding also promotes recall: for the most part, our profile of the instructional correlates of depth of understanding includes those for recall.

Clearly, how teachers treat literature—the assignments they make, the kinds of writing tasks they design, the types of discussions they conduct—does indeed affect the difficulty their students' experience with literature. It is essential to note that just as surely as all the characteristics noted in the above profiles contribute to enhanced learning, their absence will just as surely degrade it. This conclusion is sobering given Applebee's (1981) findings that the dominant uses of writing in American high school English classes are note-taking and short-answer responses, and that paragraph-length writing is "reported as a frequent activity for only 27 percent of the classes at grade nine, and 36 percent at grade eleven." In his study, 50 percent of all English teachers reported assigning short-answer exercises "frequently," whereas they assigned homework involving writing of at least a paragraph length only 10 percent of the time. In the study reported here, teachers, on average, reported asking students to write a brief essay of more than two paragraphs only about twice a month, and one page or more 1.75 times a month. (These means, and others for the variables analyzed in this study, are reported in Table 1.) As a result, it seems totally justified, in evaluating instruction in literature, to do more than ask what teachers are doing. In addition, it is important to consider and hold teachers accountable for what they are not doing: Are they or are they not assigning frequent, extensive writing? Are they or are they not engaging their students in genuine discussion that regularly transcends recitation? Are they or are they not frequently asking authentic questions? And so forth.

Many of the practices that promote depth of understanding potentially increase risk for teachers. When they ask authentic questions, for example, teachers cannot by definition fully anticipate the kinds of responses that students will make. As a result, they must be prepared to deal with a great range of possibilities, certainly greater than when they ask preplanned questions with preconceived answers. Similarly, when they encourage student discussion, teachers can never be sure exactly where it will lead. These pedagogical practices that promote depth of understanding would, therefore, seem to require depth of preparation on the part of the teacher; they should feel secure with—indeed, even relish—discussing unanticipated topics, themes, and aspects of the works they teach.

But at the same time that these practices introduce an element of risk for teachers, they also enliven instructional routines that for both students and teachers can easily become humdrum and boring. Teaching the same lesson with the same preplanned questions to three, four, or even five different classes a day can quickly dull even the most dedicated high school teacher. By contrast, managing slightly different conversations with the same classes involving the unique contributions of the different groups of students may well prove stimulating and engaging for both teachers and students, especially when the students learn that their teacher listens, takes their contributions seriously, and often follows up on them.

REFERENCES

Applebee, A. (1981). *Writing in the secondary school: English and the content areas.* Urbana, Ill.: National Council of Teachers of English.

————. (1984). "Writing and reasoning." *Review of Educational Research,* 54 (4), 577–96.

Fish, S. (1980). *Is there a text in this class?* Cambridge: Harvard University Press.

Gall, M. D. (1984). "Synthesis of research on teachers' questioning." *Educational Leadership,* 42, 40–47.

Goodlad, J. I. (1984). *A place called school.* New York: McGraw-Hill.

Hirsch, E. D., Jr. (1987). *Cultural literacy: What every American needs to know.* Boston: Houghton Mifflin.

Hoetker, J., and Ahlbrand, W. P., Jr. (1969). "The persistence of the recitation." *American Education Research Journal,* 6, 145–67.

Langer, J., and Applebee, A. (1987). *How writing shapes thinking.* Urbana, Ill.: National Council of Teachers of English.

Newmann, F. (1988). "Can depth replace coverage in the high school curriculum?" *Phi Delta Kappan,* January, 345–48.

Nystrand, M. (1986). *The structure of written communication: Studies in reciprocity between writers and readers.* Orlando and London: Academic Press.

Nystrand, M. and Gamoran, A. (1989). "Instructional discourse and student engagement." Paper presented at the 1989 convention of the American Educational Research Association.Madison: National Center on Effective Secondary Schools.

Powell, A., Farrar, E., and Cohen, D. K. (1985). *The shopping mall high school.* Boston: Houghton-Mifflin.

Rosenblatt, L. (1938). *Literature as exploration.* New York: Appleton-Century.

————. (1978). *The reader, the text, the poem: A transactional theory of the literary work.* Carbondale: Southern Illinois University Press.

Sizer, T. (1984). *Horace's compromise.* Boston: Houghton-Mifflin.

Smith, F. (1971). *Understanding reading.* New York: Holt, Rinehart, and Winston.

8.

Indeterminate Texts, Responsive Readers, and the Idea of Difficulty in Literature

Alan C. Purves

Those involved with the assessment of literature learning have long been concerned with the issue of difficulty. They have had to face the issue in their determination of what is to be tested and how, and the question of how one concludes that one student is "better" than another. Since examiners must deal with a psychometric world that seeks certainty and definitiveness of answers, reliability in the rating of performance, and the ability to rank students on a true scale from the able reader to the insensitive clod, they encounter a complex set of problems. It is the purpose of this paper to address both the dilemma that examiners face and the fundamental contradictions in the very term "examination of literary understanding."

Traditionally examiners have focused upon one of three aspects of the curriculum, depending upon which has held sway within the profession and the schools: knowledge of texts and related information (biographical information and literary terms); critical and interpretive reading performance with respect to individual texts or groups of texts, including the application of knowledge; and attitudes concerning literature and particular texts, including the affective aspects of understanding a text (Applebee, 1971; Purves, 1971, 1973; Purves and Beach, 1973).

LITERATURE LEARNING AS KNOWLEDGE

In the first and oldest view of the curriculum, literature is viewed as a school subject with its own body of knowledge. This body consists primarily of literary texts, perhaps specified by genre, date, theme, author, and other classifications. These particular texts are set in part by experts, in part by those who purvey textbooks, and in part by teachers and curriculum planners. There are three other broad areas of literature content: 1) historical and background information concerning authors, texts, and the times in which they were written, or that form their subject matter; 2) information concerning critical terminology, critical strategies, and literary theory; and 3) information of a broad cultural nature, such as that emerging from folklore and mythology, which forms a necessary starting point for the reading of many literary texts.

From the 1930s into the 1970s, many commercial tests and examinations focused upon such matters as authors and titles, as well as questions pertaining to history and to certain critical terms. Difficulty was seen as comprising increasingly recondite items and details, or it was seen as following a progression based on a determination of which texts from the canon were taught in which years of school. Addison's "Sir Roger deCoverley" would be appropriate for the junior high school, Lamb's "Elia" for the senior high school.

This perspective on literature teaching and learning has been frequently criticized as focusing too much on things external to the text. At the same time, many have argued that such factual knowledge is crucial to the acts of reading and writing. In the world of testing, there are few commercial tests that concentrate on this sort of knowledge (usually at the college level), although it formed the basis of the 1987 study of cultural knowledge (Ravitch and Finn, 1987; Applebee, Langer, and Mullis, 1987).

LITERATURE LEARNING AS READING AND WRITING

In the 1960s, there began a shift in the content of literature tests away from an emphasis on factual knowledge toward one on critical reading of texts presumed unfamiliar to the student. This shift can be thought of as the incorporation of the New Criticism into the curriculum. In some respects the move can also be seen as a politically expedient one as the canon was challenged by a variety of groups arguing for a broadening or even an elimination of any canonical approach to the literature curriculum. Those who create tests of critical reading seek to determine difficulty on some basis associated with the nature of the text, whether it be morphological, syntactic, structural, or referential. The precise combination of textual factors and a clear formula for determining difficulty has eluded most literary scholars and certainly has eluded test-makers.

This perspective on school literature has often been fitted—rather uncomfortably—into "the language arts," which are defined as reading, writing, speaking, and listening. Since literature involves texts that people read or write, and since when students read literature they often write about what they have read, literature is often seen as simply a subset of reading and writing, with an occasional nod to speaking and listening. Literature fits into the program as something pleasant to read and perhaps as something interesting to write about. This view seems to prevail in the basal reading approach to elementary schools (see Walmsley and Walp, 1989), and carries on into the secondary school curriculum. Literature is a content to promote skills in reading and writing or to promote individual growth, depending upon the ideology attached to language arts instruction. In the current world of tests, literature is often a vehicle for reading comprehension tests or for measures of writing skill and proficiency rather than a measure of the skills set forward by the New Critics or the structuralists.

LITERATURE LEARNING AS THE DEVELOPMENT OF HABITS

The third aspect of the curriculum, that concerning attitudes, interests, and habits as well as the affective component of reading and responding to literary texts, has not been covered extensively in examinations, although it has been the focus of extremely vocal groups both in and out of schools. Some of those in schools have been concerned with personal growth and development and with the "student-centered" curriculum; those out of the schools have been concerned with issues of censorship and morality. Both groups have proclaimed the importance of the development of preferred habits in reading and discourse about what has been read even though they have been on opposite sides of various political fences. These aspects of the curriculum have been difficult to measure and it has been hard to set criteria for determining difficulty and development. Many of the advocates of this kind of a curriculum have called for the abolition of tests of any sort and have chosen more "subjective" approaches to determining achievement.

This group sees the domain of literature learning as the development of a different kind of reading from that used with other texts. This kind of reading is called "aesthetic" and is opposed to the reading that one does with informational texts. Recent literary theory has come to view literature less in terms of the writer and more in terms of the reader, for it appears to be the reader, particularly the informed and trained reader, who defines a text as literary and reads it not for the information, but for the experience of the nuances of the text itself. Such a definition follows from the strand of thinking that developed from I. A. Richard's *Practical Criticism* (1929), where the idea that the reader helped form the meaning of the text was given cogent voice. The summary of the position is best expressed by Louise Rosenblatt in *The Reader, The Text, The Poem* (1978), who says that literary texts are grounded in the real world of writers who may or may not intend them to be seen poetically.

Thus a major function of literature education is the development of what one might call preferences, which is to say habits of mind in reading and writing. One must learn to read aesthetically and to switch lenses when one moves from social studies to poetry. In addition, literature education is supposed to develop something called "taste" or the love of "good literature," so that literature education goes beyond reading and writing in the inculcation of specific sets of preferred habits of reading and writing about that particular body of texts called literature. Difficulty in this view can be seen as being partly contained in the relationship between reader and text, and in the "subtlety" of discourse about the aesthetic experience.

The Current Situation

One of the studies by the Center for the Learning and Teaching of Literature comprised an analysis of the available tests in secondary school (Brody, DeMilo, and Purves, 1989). The analysis showed that for the most part the tests that contained literary passages asked questions about them as if they were the same as passages from encyclopedias. There was some testing of general literary knowledge but virtually no testing of knowledge or application of critical terminology, and virtually no testing of analysis or aesthetic judgment. One might argue that this state of affairs results from a clear victory of the reading and writing group and the triumph of the New Critics. A more cynical interpretation would have it that there is in fact a void in the testing of learning in literature because there is no strong advocate for including literature in assessment programs. Certainly there is not a clear theoretical position upon which to base a testing program that would resolve the issue of difficulty. In the remainder of this paper, I should like to attempt that task.

A FUNCTIONAL DEFINITION OF LITERATURE BASED UPON THE COMMUNITY OF READERS

Let us begin with some definitions. Texts are artifacts produced by a genus called writer or author. Texts possess in common the broad features of having a content (that subject matter or referential world with which they deal), a structure, and a set of distinctive linguistic features that are often referred to as style and tone. These three divisions are ones that readers and writers often make even though the readers and writers realize that the sum of the text is greater than the parts, and that the text may be perceived as an organic whole.

Writers may have in mind a variety of functions for the text they are writing when they write. A literary text, to the extent there is a separate type, may only be defined as the verbal expression of the writer's imagination, a definition too broad to be useful. One reason is that readers may also see a given text as having one of a number of functions as they read it, and their perception may not coincide with that of the writer. In general the range of functions tends to approximate those set forth by Jakobson (1987): metalingual, expressive, referential, conative, poetic, and phatic. In general, too, no writer or reader perceives a text as being a pure representative of a single function. The functions mix and the labels are only partial descriptors.

Recent literary theory has come to view literature less in terms of the writer and more in terms of the reader, for it appears to be the reader, particularly the informed and trained reader, who defines a text as literary. A reader may allow all sorts of works that once had been excluded or marginal (essays, letters, biographies, and the like) as a part of a literary group. Once written, texts become alive only when they are read, and they become literary when a reader chooses to read them as aesthetic objects rather than as documents.

The individual reader does not operate in a vacuum. Most readers belong to a community, a group of people who share certain common perceptions and beliefs about the function of texts in society (Fish, 1980; Purves, 1985b, 1986, 1988). These readers bring common background knowledge concerning the substance, structure, and style of the texts in order to ascertain the meaning and significance of the text. The meaning is that which can be verified by the community, perhaps with recourse to the historical grounding of the text, if such is available. The significance is personal in terms of the communal perception.

Different communities of readers tend to allocate a function to a given text as they incorporate it into a body of texts. That is, they will assign a text to a group with a similar function or genre (e.g., poem, story, literature). These communities are often related to critical schools or to critical positions that determine the literary nature of a given text. Literary texts, then, do not exist as a separate category of text that can be defined in terms of certain internal characteristics *sub specie aeternitatis*. Rather, literary texts tend to be proximally defined as those that communities perceive as literary, which is to say that they are texts that a significant number of readers read aesthetically and claim should be so read.

This theoretical position thus argues that any text has the potential of being literary should a significant group of knowledgeable and experienced readers determine that there is value in reading the text as an aesthetic object. In this way, such works as the speeches of Abraham Lincoln and Martin Luther King, Jr., the letters of John Keats and Hector St. John de Crevecoeur, and the diary of Anne Frank become literary objects and part of the canon in the United States. Readers have read them in the light of a common experience of literary texts and have derived principles of "literariness" that allow them to accept these works. In part, their criteria are formal and structural, in part they arise from consideration of the breadth of vision of the writer. However determined, there comes to exist a set of texts that the community refers to as "literature," which is to say it is to be viewed functionally as being predominantly poetic and therefore to be read aesthetically. This accretion of a canon comes particularly with the advent of formal schooling and the inclusion of mother-tongue instruction—although it had its roots in "classical" language instruction.

From this communal network of texts that grows over time and that is part of the background that weaves a community into one, comes one of the well-known features of literature—its tendency to feed upon itself as well as upon folklore, myth, and historical events (Frye, 1957; Hirsch, 1983,1987; Bakhtin, 1981). Many literary works are clearly situated in a web of culture, just as many others are situated in a specific time and place (e.g., Jonathan Swift's works, which are clearly situated in eighteenth-century England). We may argue that when writers select a given word, they do so with a penumbra of associations and references that are peculiarly theirs and their culture's, and have reference to their reading as well as their conversation and other linguistic experiences.

One of the clearest examples of this can be seen in the work of John Livingstone Lowes, who in *The Road to Xanadu* (1927) traced every line in Coleridge's "Rime of the Ancient Mariner" and "Kublai Khan" to its source in one of the hundreds of books that Coleridge had read. Literature uses allusion and many writers presume background knowledge on the part of the reader even though the allusions have been transmuted into a new artifact. Nonliterary texts also presume much of the same knowledge. But there is the difference that literary texts form part of a large textual world that is interdependent and forms that thing called literature. So the literary community determines.

The view of literature that I have set forth is that, although texts are finally indeterminate, a group of them has been set aside by communities as forming a part of the communal experience. These communities have selected them to be read aesthetically, and by virtue of that fact, the texts have developed a set of associations with each other. Subsequent writers acculturated into this "tradition" produce texts that are highly allusive to this communal set of literature. I might add that what has happened in the literary world has also happened in certain transnational disciplines such as psychology and economics. Certain texts have emerged as a core upon which other texts have built. The core in both cases challenges, and at times drops, certain writers and texts as it adds others. It is a fluid corpus, not a fixed canon; the organic metaphor is quite appropriate.

LITERATURE EDUCATION AS INDUCTION INTO THE COMMUNITY

This brings us back to the issue of the literature curriculum. It appears to have the function of bringing the individual into the community. That is to say, it appears to be aimed at providing the student with the requisite knowledge of the communal canon, as well as with the ways of reading that preserve the appropriate view of the functions of texts in the community. In Purves (1971) there was laid out a depiction of the literature curriculum in terms of content and behaviors. The content consists primarily of literary texts, which may be specified by genre, date, theme, author, and other classifications. The particular texts are set in part by experts, in part by those who purvey textbooks, and in part by teachers and curriculum planners.

There are four other broad areas of literature content: historical and background information concerning authors, texts, and the times in which they were written or that form their subject matter; information concerning critical terminology, critical strategies, and literary theory; information of a broad cultural nature such as that emerging from folklore and mythology, which forms a necessary starting point for the reading of many literary texts; and the set of critical strategies, procedures, dispositions, and routines that the community values.

One of the findings of Broudy (1982) when he sought to study how knowledge was used by readers was that the sort of learning that was used most frequently in the protocols was not what, but how. Although many readers remembered previous texts or bits of text they used to help them read a new text, in most instances the subjects had learned and applied certain "mannerisms" of reading (for want of a better word), such as one student's immediate distrust of anything that contained metaphor, or another student's manner of reading all literature that derived from the critical theory of Maritain. On subsequent interviews, the readers recalled precisely where they had learned to read certain texts in the ways that they did. Such a finding suggests a corroboration of earlier research on reader response (Purves, 1973, 1981), that readers become culturally indoctrinated into a way of reading literature that they apply to new texts that they read. They can become frustrated if the text does not stand up to the methodology they have acquired.

Another kind of learning that might eventuate from the study of literature would be the acquisition of a communal set of values concerning literature and perhaps arising from the content of the literature read. This has long been the thought of those who create literature programs in the schools as well as those who write. Shelley claimed poets were the unacknowledged legislators of humankind. Emerson sought to create an American literature that would solidify American values. The community has decided what is literature and what literature should be for the reader. The students learn to acquiesce and accept these values as they become loyal to the community.

Thus we have returned to the three views of the curriculum and examinations that we described in the first part of the paper, but in doing so we see that these are complementary and inextricably intertwined rather than being options from which to choose. We would argue that the domain of school literature can be divided into three interrelated aspects: *knowledge, practice,* and *preferred habit.* The interrelationships are complex in that one uses knowledge in the various acts that constitute the practice and the preferred habits, and that the practices and preferred habits can have their influence on knowledge. At the same time, one can separate them for the purposes of curriculum planning and, as we shall see, testing. We may schematize the three subdomains as follows:

SCHOOL LITERATURE

KNOWLEDGE		PRACTICE		PREFERRED HABIT	
Textual	Extratextual	Responding	Articulating	Aesthetic Choice	Habits of Behavior
Specific text	History	Decoding	Retelling	Evaluating	Reading
Cultural Allusion	Author	Envisioning	Discussing single works	Selecting	Criticizing
	Genres	Analyzing		Valuing	
	Styles	Personalizing	Generalizing across works		
	Critical terms	Interpreting			

I have omitted under the first group the sorts of knowledge that are requisite to the reading of any text (Purves, 1984, 1985a, 1988) (which is to say knowledge of the lexicon and grammatical and text structures) and have concentrated on that body of knowledge that appears to distinguish literature as a separate and perhaps unique domain. Knowledge of texts can be contained in texts, myths, and folktales, or it can exist outside texts as part of the common core. Many people know about a "Romeo" without having read the play.

Under practice, *responding* includes reading, watching, and listening. It includes decoding or making out the plain sense of the text or film, envisioning or coming to some whole impression and re-creation of what is read, and the more detailed aspects of analyzing, personalizing, and interpreting. Often people envision without analyzing or interpreting. The term *articulating* covers a wide variety of ways by which students let people know what their response is. Articulation is central to the curriculum in many ways, because like any school subject, literature involves public acts in which the student must be more articulate about procedures and strategies as well as conclusions, than might be true of the subject outside school. Proofs are not necessary in mathematical applications outside school; essays about one's reading of a text are not required after reading every library book. It is in the articulation as well as the display of knowledge and preferred habits that the student comes into contact with the community and is accepted into it. It is hoped that the articulation of a response will come to influence the response itself (Purves, 1971).

In order to preserve the aesthetic nature of the text, and treat the work of literature as literature, not as a treatise on whales, the curriculum seeks to inculcate a communal set of preferred habits. If literary works are not read and talked about as other kinds of texts are read, but are read differently, students must learn how to perform this kind of reading and they must be encouraged to read this way voluntarily. The curriculum then must seek to promote habits of mind in reading and writing. One of these habits is to make aesthetic judgments about the various texts read, and to justify these judgments publicly. Personal preference is not sufficient to the curriculum, one must learn to be a critic in the sense of a judge.

Literature education, then, is supposed to develop something called "taste" or the love of "good literature," so that literature education goes beyond reading and writing, and specific sets of preferred habits of reading and writing. It may include the development of a tolerance for the variety of literature, a willingness to acknowledge that many different kinds and styles of work can be thought of as literature, and an acceptance that just because we do not like a certain poem, does not mean that it is not good. It can even lead students to distrust the meretricious or the shoddy use of sentiment. Experienced readers of literature can see that they are being tricked by a book or a film even when the trickery is going on—and they can enjoy the experience.

DIFFICULTY REDEFINED

If we redefine learning in literature as has been outlined, so that it involves the intersection of knowledge, practice, and preferred habits, and, so that the standards for learning being achieved are those of the community into which a given individual is entering, the nature of difficulty is resolved as being a combination of: 1) the complexity and detail of requisite knowledge to be a member of the community; 2) the use of that knowledge in responding and articulating a response; and 3) the use of that knowledge in the making of appropriate aesthetic judgments and distinctions between personal and communal standards in the exercise of preferences and habitual behaviors with respect to texts. Such a definition also allows for works to be difficult, based not on some intrinsic characteristics, but in terms of their community. Shakespeare may be harder or easier depending upon the nature of the community and its standards concerning knowledge, practice, and preferred habits, and upon the intellectual distance an individual must travel to enter that community.

The difficulty of a text (D), then, varies with the amount of knowledge (K) presumed by the community sufficient for an individual to demonstrate an adequate (A) and appropriate (A^1) articulation of a response to that text:

$$D = K (A + A^1)$$

Thus no text is easy or difficult outside the norms and standards of the community that determines: 1) what is necessary and sufficient knowledge; 2) what is an adequately framed discussion of that text or generalization about the text within a larger discussion of literature; and 3) what is an appropriate aesthetic disposition toward the text.

We can illustrate this principle with the following text as an example:

Buffalo Bill's
defunct
      who used to
      ride a watersmooth-silver
                        stallion
and break onetwothreefourfive pigeonsjustlikethat
                                    Jesus
he was a handsome man
                  and what i want to know is
how do you like your blueeyed boy
Mister Death
                              —e.e. cummings

In terms of knowledge, the difficulty of this poem depends upon the degree to which the community deems it important to know who Buffalo Bill was, the background and poetics of Cummings, and Cummings's place in twentieth-century American poetry. A group of students can show understanding of the text with a vague knowledge of each of these points. To demand a more precise knowledge immediately makes the poem more difficult. Thus the poem is perhaps easier for a high school class than it might be at the university level.

As it is with knowledge, so it is with practice. The community may require an elaborated discussion of the style and structure of the poem as it relates to an interpretation that deals with the death of a superstar and the views that the American public had of Buffalo Bill, as well as Cummings's ambivalence toward American heroes, the American public, and death. On the other hand, the text could be simply presented to a group of readers with a request for a minimal articulation of a response to the poem, perhaps only a request to identify the author or the period or to read it aloud. If the elaborated knowledge needs to be further integrated into an appropriately detailed essay with proof and counters to alternative interpretations, the poem takes on an additional layer of difficulty.

If one were to add to that the demand that the reader also elaborate an aesthetic judgment of the poem so as to demonstrate an awareness of the norms of reading modern American poetry, and acquiescence to the habit of reading poetry in such a way as to evince delight in the experience, the difficulty of the text increases. If, however, the reader were only asked to comment on a personal judgment as in "Did you like it?" the difficulty is not great.

The difficulty of a literary text, then, is only partially determined by various characteristics of the text itself. Much more influential are the demands placed by the community upon its members concerning that text. The community may demand a more or less elaborate articulation of the individual reader's knowledge and understanding of the poem, and may set detailed criteria to judge that articulation and the degree to which it satisfies the community's ideal of an aesthetic reading. Just as the community establishes the literary qualities of a text and its canonicity, so it establishes the criteria by which the text's difficulty may be determined. A text's difficulty depends upon the nature of the understanding expected. For this reason, a poem like "The Wasteland" is difficult when a reader is expected to elaborate all the interconnections, ambiguities, and allusions, and make a coherent statement about the poem. The poem is complex because a group of readers has established the ground rules for complexity; if they were to take a more impressionistic view of how the poem is to be read, its complexity diminishes.

THE IMPLICATIONS FOR ASSESSMENT

From this revised view of the curriculum in literature and the consequent idea of difficulty, those concerned with assessment can derive a set of principles by which to select texts, questions concerning texts, and criteria for judging answers to the questions. We see that the text, question, and criterion are inseparable as determinants of the difficulty of a text. We can perhaps apply the formula $D = K (A + A^1)$ to various combinations as they appear in examinations. At the simplest level, we can argue that a text accompanied by multiple-choice questions should be less difficult than the same text accompanied by an essay question. The main reason for this is that with the multiple-choice question, the answers are already there and the students do not need to generate their own language (see Hansson in this volume).

We can also argue that a text such as "Buffalo Bill's defunct" would be easier were the essay question to call upon a greater amount of technical or historical knowledge than if the students were simply to write about their feelings or understanding of the poem. That question could, however, become difficult if the scoring criterion were to be such that the students had to demonstrate a sophisticated writing style or had to match the aesthetic judgment of the adult community seeing this as a classic example of a valid early modern ironic free-verse poem, and not as something so simpleminded that a child could have written it. The difficulty of the poem becomes greater for the graduate student than for the high school senior.

CONCLUSION

I do not think that what has been set forth is sufficient to establish an inexorable calculus of textual difficulty. On the contrary, the definition of difficulty I have posited is highly situational and is clearly related to the intersection of the text, the student, and the community. Such situational difficulty is not unlike the definition of interplay of the communal and individual reponse suggested in my earlier work (Purves, 1985a). There I suggested that the community of readers that the student-reader inhabits (or is in the process of entering) determines something of the student's response to the poem and thus helps to explain the commonality of readings of a text within a community, as well as the individuality that may occur within that community. The same interplay between individual and community helps to determine the difficulty of a text for the individual. Although texts may be indeterminate, they are not so within a community unless the community so stipulates. The educational system is a communal arrangement and so establishes commonality of interpretation as well as common standards of knowledge, practice, and preferred habits in reading. These common standards may shift as the community becomes more and more esoteric.

The examiner's dilemma as posed at the beginning of this paper may not be solved, but the problems, I believe, are clarified. An examination is something determined with reference to the community of readers into which the individual or the class is being led. In literature, this means that its content and its criteria are communal; so too is the definition of difficulty of a given literary text.

REFERENCES

Applebee, A. N. (1971). *Tradition and reform in the teaching of English.* Urbana, Ill.: National Council of Teachers of English.

Applebee, A. N., Langer, J. L., and Mullis, I. (1987). *Literature and history.* Princeton, N.J.: National Assessment of Educational Progress.

Bakhtin, M. (1981). *The dialogic imagination.* M. Holquist, ed., C. Caryl and M. Holquist, trans. Austin: University of Texas Press.

Brody, P., DeMilo, C., and Purves A. (1989). *The current state of assessment in literature.*(Report series 3.1). Albany, N.Y.: Center for the Learning and Teaching of Literature.

Broudy, H. (1982). "Report: On case studies on uses of knowledge." Chicago: Spencer Foundation (ERIC ED 224016).

Fish, S. (1980). *Is there a text in this class? The authority of interpretive communities.* Cambridge: Harvard University Press.

Frye, N. (1957). *Anatomy of criticism.* Princeton: Princeton University Press.

Hirsch, E. D., Jr. (1983). "Cultural literacy." *The American Scholar* (Spring): 159–69.

———. (1987). *Cultural literacy.* Boston: Houghton Mifflin.

Jakobson, R. (1987). *Language in literature.* Cambridge: Harvard University Press.

Langer, J. (1989). *The process of understanding literature.* (Report series 2.1). Albany, N.Y.: Center for the Learning and Teaching of Literature.

Lowes, J. L. (1927). *The road to Xanadu: A study in the ways of the imagination.* Boston: Houghton Mifflin.

Purves, A. C. (1971). "Evaluation of learning in literature." In B. S. Bloom, J. T. Hastings, and G. Madaus, eds., *Handbook of formative and summative evaluation of student learning.* New York: McGraw-Hill.

———. (1973). *Literature education in ten countries: An empirical study: International studies in evaluation.* Stockholm: Almqvist and Wiksell.

———. (1981). *Achievement in reading and literature: The United States in international perspective.* Urbana, Ill.: National Council of Teachers of English.

———. (1984). "The potential and real achievement of U.S. students in school reading." *American Journal of Education,* 93, 82–106.

———. (1985a). "That sunny dome; those caves of ice." In C. R. Cooper, ed., *Researching response to literature and the teaching of literature: Points of departure.* Norwood, N.J.: Ablex.

———. (1985b). "Developing rhetorical and interpretive communities." In M. Maguire and A. Paré, eds. *Patterns of development.* Montreal: Canadian Council of Teachers of English.

———. (1986). "The IEA literature and composition studies and their elucidation of the nature and formation of interpretive and rhetorical communities." *International educational research: Papers in honor of Torsten Husén*. Oxford: Pergamon Press.

Purves, A. C. (1988). "Literacy, culture and community." In D. Wagner, ed. *The future of literacy in a changing world*. Oxford: Pergamon Press.

Purves, A. C., and Beach, R. (1973). *Literature and the reader*. Urbana, Ill.: National Council of Teachers of English.

Ravitch, D., and Finn, C. E., Jr. (1987). *What seventeen-year-olds know*. Boston: Houghton Mifflin.

Richards, I. A. (1929). *Practical criticism*. New York: Harcourt Brace.

Rosenblatt, L. M. (1978). *The reader, the text, the poem: The transactional theory of the literary work*. Carbondale: Southern Illinois University Press.

Walmsley, S., and Walp, T. P. (1989). *Teaching literature in elementary school: A report of a project on the elementary school antecedents of secondary school literature instruction* (Report Series 1.3). Albany, N.Y.: Center for the Learning and Teaching of Literature.

CONTRIBUTORS

Hazard Adams is Professor of English and Comparative Literature at the University of Washington.

Wallace Chafe is Professor of Linguistics at the University of California, Santa Barbara.

Helen Regueiro Elam is Associate Professor of English at The University at Albany, State University of New York.

Gunnar Hansson is Professor Emeritus of Communication at the University of Linköping, Sweden.

Susan Hynds is Associate Professor of English Education at Syracuse University.

Martin Nystrand is Professor of English at The University of Wisconsin.

Alan Purves is Professor of Education and the Humanities at The University at Albany, State University of New York.

William Touponce is Associate Professor of English at Indiana University–Purdue University at Indianapolis.